IRISH RAILWAYS

IN THE 1950s AND 1960s

A JOURNEY THROUGH TWO DECADES

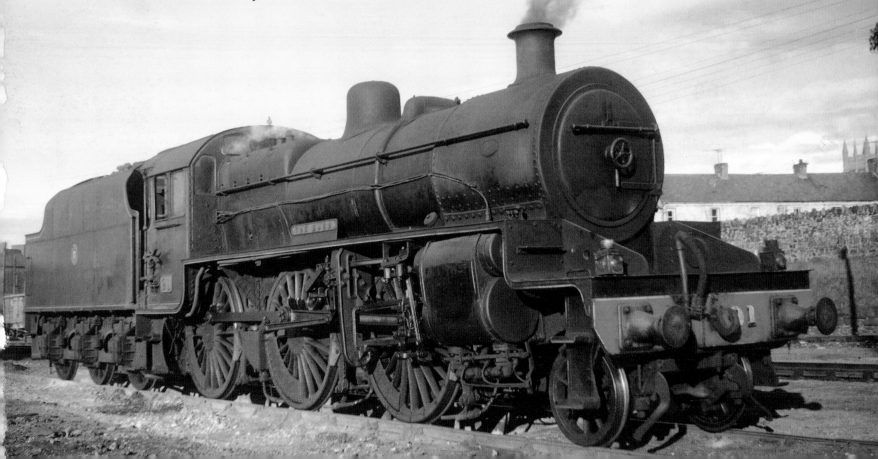

IRISH RAILWAYS

IN THE 1950s AND 1960s

A JOURNEY THROUGH TWO DECADES

KEVIN McCORMACK

PEN & SWORD
TRANSPORT

First published in Great Britain in 2017 by
Pen & Sword Transport
An imprint of Pen & Sword Books Ltd
47 Church Street
Barnsley
South Yorkshire
S70 2AS

ISBN 9781473871984

Printed and bound by Replika Press Pvt. Ltd

Pen & Sword Books Ltd incorporates the imprints of Pen & Sword Archaeology, Atlas,
Aviation, Battleground, Discovery, Family History, History, Maritime, Military, Naval,
Politics, Railways, Select, Social History, Transport, True Crime, and Claymore Press,
Frontline Books, Leo Cooper, Praetorian Press, Remember When, Seaforth Publishing
and Wharncliffe.

For a complete list of Pen & Sword titles please contact
Pen & Sword Books Limited
47 Church Street, Barnsley, South Yorkshire, S70 2AS, England
E-mail: enquiries@pen-and-sword.co.uk
Website: www.pen-and-sword.co.uk

Front cover: Former GNR(I) U class 4-4-0 No.199, *Lough Derg*, prepares to depart from Dublin Amiens Street in July 1959. Built by Beyer, Peacock in April 1915, this engine was transferred on 1 October 1958 to CIE (the last letter of which is visible stencilled in white on the bufferbeam) upon the demise of the GNR Board and was withdrawn in November 1962. The locomotive received its name in April 1949. *(Donald Nevin)*

Rear cover: County Donegal Railway diesel railcar No.18 stands at Strabane, Co Tyrone, in 1953. Entering service in 1940, this railcar was rebuilt following serious fire damage in 1949. Restored by the North West of Ireland Railway Society in 1996, it is currently on loan to the Fintown Railway in Co Donegal and operates on part of its former railway alongside Lough Finn. *(W E Robertson/Online Transport Archive)*

Title page: UTA W class 2-6-0 No.91, *The Bush*, simmers at Portadown shed, Co Armagh, in May 1962. The locomotive, which bears the name of a local river, was the second member of the W class (numbered 90-104) and was built at the Derby Works of the LMS, being delivered to the NCC in July 1933. It was scrapped in May 1965. *(Jim Oatway)*

Introduction

This album of colour photographs depicts the railway scene across Ireland during the final two full decades of steam operation. However, a review of this period would not be complete without the inclusion of a limited amount of non-steam traction, much of it relatively vintage in itself.

This book does not purport to cover the complicated history of Irish standard-gauge and narrow-gauge railways, which has already been fully covered in other publications. The purpose of this volume is to present more than 170 colour photographs that hopefully have never previously been seen in print. Indeed, it serves as a reminder of what many railway enthusiasts in Great Britain were missing across the Irish Sea, given their pre-occupation with the closure of lines under the 'Beeching Axe' and the demise of steam on British Railways. The engines and rolling stock in Ireland were generally very 'British' in appearance and part of the fascination was that most of the locomotives, even the main line ones, were comparatively small, with several having unusual wheel arrangements for their type; they looked dated (and in many cases were actually old).

A particular anomaly about Irish railways is the standard gauge, which is 5ft 3ins, as opposed to that in Great Britain which is 4ft 8^{1}/$_{2}$ins, thereby requiring any stock transferred between Great Britain and Ireland to be regauged. The narrow gauge was generally 3ft. The Irish railway companies referred to the 5ft 3ins gauge as broad gauge, but I have taken the view that the only broad gauge in Ireland was the Ulster Railway's short-lived 6ft 2ins gauge, so in this book I refer to the Irish gauge as standard gauge. In 1836 the Ulster Railway was authorised to build to a gauge of 6ft 2ins, and constructed their line from Belfast Great Victoria Street to Portadown to this gauge, whereas the Dublin and Drogheda Railway intended to use 5ft 2ins for economy reasons. Clearly, the line from Belfast to Dublin needed to have the same gauge to operate efficiently, so a compromise gauge of 5ft 3ins (hardly a compromise, some would say!) was decreed by Parliament and the Ulster Railway had to replace its broad gauge.

It is worth mentioning that the island of Ireland, consisting of thirty-two counties, used to be part of the United Kingdom. Partition occurred in 1921, when Northern Ireland was created, and a separate Irish Free State (now the Republic of Ireland) was established in the following year. The Free State controlled twenty-six counties, whereas the other six counties (Antrim, Armagh, Down, Fermanagh, Londonderry and Tyrone) remained part of the Union. Over the years there has been much restructuring of the railways on both sides of the border and the most relevant changes are summarised next.

In 1925 the various railways operating exclusively in the Free State were grouped into Great Southern Railways

(GSR), and those operating entirely in Northern Ireland were already mostly integrated into a body known as the Northern Counties Committee (NCC) owned by England's Midland Railway, which was superseded, following the railway grouping in 1923, by the London, Midland and Scottish Railway (LMS). GSR was taken over by the newly formed Coras Iompair Eireann (CIE) in 1945, and the Ulster Transport Authority (UTA), having taken control of the Belfast & County Down Railway (BCDR) in 1948, subsumed the NCC in 1949, following fifteen months of ownership by the British Transport Commission. For completeness, CIE ceased to be an operating company in 1987 and the Republic's railways are now run by a subsidiary, Iarnrod Eireann (Irish Rail). UTA's railway interests were transferred to a new body, Northern Ireland Railways (NIR), in 1968 and now branded as Translink.

The partition of Ireland raised the question of how to deal with the various railways that straddled the border. Three of these are covered in this book: two standard-gauge railways (the Great Northern Railway (Ireland) (GNR(I)) and the Sligo, Leitrim & Northern Counties Railway (SLNCR)) and one narrow-gauge (the County Donegal Railways Joint Committee (CDRJC)). The GNR was a favourite of railway enthusiasts for several reasons: it was a mainline operator whose services included the important Belfast–Dublin line, its passenger locomotives were painted sky-blue and it had two tram systems: the electric Hill of Howth Tramway in Co Dublin and the Fintona horse tram in Co Tyrone, Northern Ireland. These three railway companies were excluded from the nationalisation that occurred in Northern Ireland and the Republic in 1948 and 1950 respectively.

However, the GNR(I) suffered financial failure in the early 1950s due to increased road competition despite a modernisation programme; it announced that it was closing. This galvanised the two governments into action, culminating in de facto nationalisation by the creation of a joint governmental Board (the GNR Board) in 1953 to run the company. Outwardly, this allowed the GNR(I) to continue comparatively unchanged for a few more years until the Board was disbanded on 1 October 1958. At that point the routes and assets including the locomotives and rolling stock were divided between the UTA and CIE, although GNR(I) livery remained in evidence for a time. The division of the GNR(I) had, however, a significant impact on both sides of the border. CIE had all but abandoned steam in 1958 in favour of diesels and then found itself with an expanded rail network and some eighty extra steam locomotives, resulting in steam lingering on in the Republic until 1963. In Northern Ireland, which adopted an anti-railway approach at that time, several lines had been closed in the 1950s and the process continued with much of the inherited ex-GNR(I) network. Closure seemed to be favoured over modernisation, with the consequence that Northern Ireland was behind the Republic in terms of the steam-to-diesel transition and did not withdraw its last steam locomotives until 1970.

By this time, the Railway Preservation Society of Ireland (RPSI), formed in 1964, was gaining momentum and running railtours throughout Ireland, as it continues to do today using its fleet of preserved locomotives. Other preservation societies have also sprung up across Ireland such as the diesel-orientated Irish Traction Group and some heritage railways, with the result that a reasonable cross-section of steam and diesel motive power survives, although there are some sad omissions.

As for the other cross-border railways featured in this

This is a view from the footplate of GNR(I) U class No.199, *Lough Derg*, as it heads north out of Dublin on its way to Belfast in July 1959. *(Donald Nevin)*

book, the CDRJC was jointly run by the GNR(I) and the Midland Railway-owned NCC (later UTA) and closed in 1959. The SL & NCR, a private company latterly subsidised by the two governments, closed in 1957.

In terms of organising the photographs in this book, it was tempting to put GNR(I) locomotives and workings into a separate section, distinguishing these from CIE and UTA/NIR activities. However, most of the images of GNR(I) locomotives and trains date from the cessation of the GNR Board in 1958 and are therefore operated by the UTA or CIE, even though many locomotives still have the appearance of belonging to the Board. The book has been divided into two sections, based on whether the photographs were taken in Northern Ireland (where the main body of the book starts) or the Republic of Ireland. GNR Board and ex-GNR(I) locomotives and trains therefore appear in either section, depending on the location of the picture. With regards to the CDRJC and the SL&NCR, since most of the images of these cross-border railways were taken in Northern Ireland, and so that is the part of the book where they can be found. Northern Ireland images start at Belfast and proceed roughly in an anti-clockwise direction as far as Newry. Then we cross the border to Dundalk and move approximately in a clockwise direction through the Republic. An index of locations can be found on the last page.

As regards the photographic material itself, most has been supplied by the Online Transport Archive, a charity set up to preserve for posterity photographs and moving images of transport subjects. Some pictures have been supplied by distinguished transport photographers Roy Hobbs, Bruce Jenkins and Fred Ivey. Pictures taken by Charles Firminger, Peter Grace, James L. Stevenson and Alex Hamilton have been kindly provided by Robert

Bridger, John Laker, Hamish Stevenson and Leo Sullivan respectively. Thanks are also due to Ernie Brack and the Light Rail Transit Association (London Area) (LRTA) for the use of images in their collections and additionally, in the case of Leo Sullivan, for obtaining pictures taken by Donald Nevin.

Following the preparation of this book for publication the collection of Neil Davenport and the LRTA now belong to the Online Transport Archive.

There is a wealth of material on Irish railways both on the internet and in the many previous books on the subject but, for my research, I have found three very comprehensive tomes published by Colourpoint Books particularly useful: *Locomotives of the GNRI* by Norman Johnston, *Locomotives of the LMS/NCC* by William Scott and *Locomotives of the GSR* by Jeremy Clements and Michael McMahon.

I hope that I have captured the quirkiness and charm of the Irish railway scene in the 1950s and 1960s and that readers will derive as much enjoyment from this album as I have had in compiling it.

Kevin R. McCormack
Ashtead, Surrey
April 2016

It seems appropriate to start the Northern Ireland section in the capital, Belfast, so this is Great Victoria Street station in May 1962. The locomotive, probably acting as station pilot, is ex-GNR(I) T1 class 4-4-2 tank No.187X, built by Beyer, Peacock in 1913 for the GNR(I) and transferred to the UTA in 1958. There were five T1 class locomotives and No.187X outlived the other four by four years, not being withdrawn until April 1964 despite acquiring the 'X' suffix that meant, in effect, 'do not resuscitate' if a serious ailment occurred. As illustrated here, a feature of many of these pictures is the friendly nature of the railway employees epitomised by their desire to pose for the photographer.
(Jim Oatway)

Still carrying blue livery, UTA U class 4-4-0 No.64 (formerly GNR(I) No.196, *Lough Gill*) prepares to leave Great Victoria Street station on 16 June 1959. A Beyer, Peacock product dating from 1915, this locomotive was an early withdrawal in October 1961. The station closed in April 1976, by which time much of it had already been demolished, being replaced by a new Belfast Central station. However, a new Great Victoria Street station was opened in 1995, almost on the site of the previous station. *(C. Carter/Online Transport Archive)*

When steel-panelled stock arrived on the GNR(I), the company applied imitation wood graining to match the scumbled mahogany finish of its wooden stock, as evidenced here on 19 October 1957. At this time, the joint-governmental Board was still running the GNR(I) and the coat of arms of the original company remained unchanged apart from an alteration to the wording from 'Great Northern Railway Ireland' to 'Great Northern Railway Board'. The shield continued to show the arms of Dublin (top left), Londonderry (top right), Enniskillen (lower left) and Belfast (lower right) with the Red Hand of Ulster in the centre. *(W.E. Robertson/Online Transport Archive)*

GNR(I) No.1 shunts stock at Great Victoria Street station on 19 October 1957. This T2 class 4-4-2 tank was built by Beyer, Peacock in 1921, transferred to CIE in 1958 and withdrawn in October 1959. The building in the background with pinnacles is the New Fisherwick Presbyterian Church built in 1905. Great Victoria Street station was the centrally located Belfast terminus of the GNR(I) and was served by Adelaide depot in South Belfast. York Road station was the NCC's Belfast terminus, with York Road locomotive depot and works located close by. The city's third main station was the former Belfast & County Down Railway terminus at Queen's Quay, which latterly only operated services to Bangor. Like Great Victoria Street, it was subsequently replaced by Belfast Central station in 1976. *(W.E. Robertson/Online Transport Archive)*

More shunting at Great Victoria Street station on 19 October 1957, this time featuring GNR(I) Q class 4-4-0 No.131 (named *Uranus* until 1914), attached to GNR(I) railcar stock. The locomotive was built in 1901 by Neilson Reid of Glasgow, the company becoming part of the newly formed North British Company in 1903. The thirteen members of the Q class were built between 1899 and 1904 and No.131 enjoyed a long working life, being transferred to CIE in 1958 and not withdrawn until October 1963, whereupon it was preserved by CIE as a static exhibit. The engine is now in the hands of the Railway Preservation Society of Ireland (RPSI), which returned it to steam in 2015 after more than fifty years of inactivity. *(W.E. Robertson/Online Transport Archive)*

The GNR(I) was the first Irish railway company to introduce dining cars and is said to have been the first in the British Isles to have electric lighting in all of its passenger coaches. The company provided restaurant cars on its express services between Belfast and Londonderry and Belfast to Dublin, which were particularly popular among passengers travelling to sporting events. This view from a passing train on 19 October 1957 outside Great Victoria Street station depicts an elderly restaurant car in the company's familiar orange-brown livery. A more modern ex-GNR(I) restaurant car, No.88, built in 1938, still runs on the mainline, forming part of the RPSI's Dublin-based heritage set, but this carries CIE green livery to match the rest of the rolling stock. *(W.E. Robertson/Online Transport Archive)*

Fortune shined on this dilapidated UTA (ex-GNR(I)) vehicle pictured at Grosvenor Road goods yard, adjacent to Great Victoria Street station, in August 1964, for it now stands resplendent in the Ulster Folk and Transport Museum at Cultra, Co Down. Built originally as a normal bus, registration ZI 2452, in 1928, it became Railbus E in October 1934 following the fitting of GNR(I)-patented Howden-Meredith wheels (a pneumatic tyre within a steel outer rim). However, normal wagon wheels were later fitted to the front axle because the pneumatic tyres could not operate the signalling track circuits. Subsequently renumbered in succession E2, 1 and finally 8178, and rebodied and re-engined in 1947, this converted bus was used as an inspection vehicle from 1958 until its withdrawal in 1963. You can see this vehicle in its guise of GNR(I) No.1 on pages 94 and 95. *(Marcus Eavis/Online Transport Archive)*

This scene at Belfast Docks in July 1959 depicts ex-GNR(I) RT class 0-4-4 tank No.23. It was unique in being the only locomotive to enter the UTA's capital stock (that is, excluding those with an 'X' suffix) and retain the same number following acquisition in 1958. There were four members of this class, all built by Beyer, Peacock, and No.23 dated from 1908. They were built as dock shunters specifically to work in Belfast, for which purpose they were fitted with reduced boiler mountings, a wheelbase designed for tight curves and a large bunker for a day's supply of coal. All four passed to the UTA and three, including No.23, survived until 1963. *(Donald Nevin)*

The LMS influence is clearly evident in this view of NCC U2 class 4-4-0 No.84, *Lisanoure Castle*, at York Road, Belfast in July 1959. This type of locomotive was very similar in appearance to the LMS class 2P 4-4-0s and since none of these locomotives survived into preservation, it is fortunate that a U2, No.74, *Dunluce Castle,* was saved and is displayed at Cultra. The U2 class, which numbered eighteen machines, were nicknamed the 'Scotch engines' because seven were built by North British, although the remainder, including No.84, were built at the NCC's workshops at York Road. This locomotive was in fact a rebuild of A class 4-4-0 No.20 in 1929, the original machine dating from 1905. *(Donald Nevin)*

Still on 19 October 1957, two railwaymen enjoy the delights of al fresco travel in the autumn sunshine as NCC U2 class 4-4-0 No.80, *Dunseverick Castle*, steams forth with goods wagons at York Road, Belfast. This engine was built at York Road in 1925 and withdrawn in December 1961. That was the final year in which the U2s saw service; increasing dieselisation led to a reduction in the need for steam locomotives, which was adequately met by the newer NCC Moguls and 'Jeep' tanks, as well as more modern ex-GNR(I) engines acquired in 1958. *(W.E. Robertson/Online Transport Archive)*

The ornate NCC livery is epitomised in this study of V1 class 0-6-0 No.15 at York Road shed, Belfast. Completed at Derby in 1923 as V class No.73 and almost immediately exchanging identities with U class 4-4-0 No.15, the locomotive was rebuilt with a Belpaire boiler in 1953, whereupon it was reclassified from V to V1. There were only three members of this class and No.15 survived until 1961. This picture was another to be taken on 19 October 1957. Although regarded as heavy goods engines, they were often used on local passenger trains and No.15 was loaned to the GNR Board for four months in 1956. *(W.E. Robertson/Online Transport Archive)*

Ireland was quick to see savings that could arise from the replacement of steam traction by diesel on passenger services and UTA started this process with the introduction into service of Multi-Engine Diesel units (MEDs) in 1951. These were followed by more powerful Multi-Purpose Diesel units (MPDs) built from 1957-1962. Here we see one of the initial batch of single-cab power cars, MPD No.37, on 19 October 1957 approaching York Road station with the locomotive depot's coaling plant visible in the distance. This diesel unit was converted from steam-hauled stock and fitted with a Leyland underfloor engine but was later re-engined. The term 'Multi-Purpose Diesel' was a reference to the fact that these units were sufficiently powerful to take on the duties of a small diesel locomotive, such as hauling goods wagons or shunting. *(W.E. Robertson/Online Transport Archive)*

Harland & Woolf of Belfast is well known as a ship builder, but it was also the only Irish company to build diesel locomotives. UTA acquired four Harland diesels and this view at York Road depot on 9 June 1957 depicts X class 0-6-0 No.17. This was a powerful shunting locomotive of 330bhp with a tractive effort of 24,000lbs. Built in 1937, the machine was initially hired by the NCC and purchased in 1941. It was withdrawn about 1966 and scrapped a few years later. *(Paul de Beer/Online Transport Archive)*

This picture depicts another UTA diesel shunter, also standing at York Road depot on 9 June 1957. Another Harland & Woolf product, this 0-4-0 of 225bhp was designed as a shunter for their dockyard in 1937 and borrowed by the NCC in 1945-46. The locomotive joined the NCC fleet permanently in 1951, becoming No.16 following the withdrawal of the steam 0-4-0 saddle tank dock shunter of 1914 vintage that previously carried this number and had latterly worked at York Road depot. No.16 was withdrawn about 1965. *(Paul de Beer/Online Transport Archive)*

NCC U2 class 4-4-0 No.72 stands over the ash pit at York Road depot in June 1957. This locomotive was one of six out of the class of eighteen not to carry a name because, although it was allocated the name *Shane's Castle*, the W class 2-6-0s had arrived by the time No.72 emerged, and that class (apart from two) was favoured to receive names instead. No.72 was the penultimate member of the class to appear, being rebuilt at York Road from U class 4-4-0 No.72 in February 1937. For some six months in 1954, it was hired by the GNR Board, mainly working cross-border trains between Belfast and Clones, Co Monaghan. *(Nick Nicolson/The Transport Treasury)*

Destined for a preserved future at the RPSI's base at Whitehead, UTA Z class 0-6-4 tank No.27, *Lough Erne*, appears in fine fettle at York Road depot. This was one of two such locomotives (the other appears on page 65) bought by the UTA from Beyer, Peacock upon the closure of the Sligo, Leitrim & Northern Counties Railway (SLNCR) in 1957. The SLNCR had ordered these engines in 1949 but could not afford to pay for them, so they remained under the ownership of Beyer, Peacock on loan to the SLNCR under a form of hire purchase agreement. The UTA latterly used the engines as shunters at Belfast Docks. *(Ernie's Railway Archive)*

The NCC was created in 1903 out of the Belfast & Northern Counties Railway. With that company came its Locomotive Superintendent, Bowman Malcolm, who had been appointed to that position in 1876. Malcolm's last locomotive design was the V class superheated heavy goods 0-6-0s, which consisted of three engines, latterly numbered 13, 14 and 15, delivered from Derby in January 1923. No.13, seen here at York Road depot on 10 May 1962, received a reconditioned boiler in 1938, whereupon it was reclassified from V class to V1. No.14 and No.15 (*see page 19*) were withdrawn in 1961 but No.13 lasted another three years. *(Jim Oatway)*

Left: This withdrawn locomotive, UTA Y class 0-6-0 tank No.19X, is an ex-LMS Fowler 'Jinty', one of 422 built and, had it not been sold to the NCC in 1944, would have become BR No.47553. Along with UTA No.18 (ex-LMS No.7456), it was regauged and dispatched to the NCC to help fill a shortage of suitable shunting engines during the Second World War. Initially, this need was met by the purchase from the GNR(I) in 1942 of three ancient former Dundalk, Newry & Greenore Railway 0-6-0 saddletanks but these had proved unsatisfactory. Jinty No.18 was withdrawn in 1956 but No.19 remained in service until 1962, shortly before this picture was taken at York Road shed on 10 May 1962.

Above: The wheels have come off UTA 4-4-0 No.66 at York Road Works on 10 May 1962. Previously GNR(I) No.201, *Meath*, this U class engine was built by Beyer, Peacock in 1947, transferred to UTA in 1958 and withdrawn in May 1965. *(Jim Oatway – both)*

Left: Moving across Belfast on 10 May 1962 to the former GNR(I) depot at Adelaide, UTA No.49, unlike No.66 on the previous page, does not enjoy the benefit of covered accommodation when lifted by a crane for the removal of its wheels. The locomotive is a UG class 0-6-0 built by Beyer, Peacock in February 1948 and withdrawn in January 1967. **Above:** This view of Adelaide depot in July 1964 finds two ex-GNR(I) locomotives on shed together with newly overhauled NCC/UTA 'Jeep' 2-6-4 tank No.55. The ex-GNR(I) engines are S class 4-4-0s originally built by Beyer, Peacock in 1913: UTA No.60, *Slieve Donard*, (formerly GNR(I) No.172) and UTA No.170, *Errigal*. The latter has retained its GNR(I) number under UTA ownership because, unlike No.172, it was transferred to CIE on cessation of the GNR Board in 1958 and was only acquired by UTA in 1963, at which stage renumbering was not considered worthwhile. *(Jim Oatway; Marcus Eavis/Online Transport Archive)*

These two pictures were taken in August 1962 at the former GNR(I) Adelaide depot, which opened in 1911 and closed in October 1966. A maintenance facility for diesel trains has since been built on the site but, in recognition of its former use, the train used to convey VIPs from Belfast Central for the opening ceremony on 12 December 2012 (12/12/12!) was hauled by the RPSI's J15 0-6-0 No.186. The locomotives seen in the pictures here are: **left:** UTA S2 class 4-4-0 No.63, formerly GNR(I) No.192, *Slievenamon*, built by Beyer, Peacock in 1915 and withdrawn in May 1965; and **above:** a 'Jeep' 2-6-4 tank standing alongside an ex-GNR(I) Glover 4-4-2 tank. The latter is believed to be No.5X, which was the only UTA class T2 locomotive not to have been withdrawn before 1962. *(Fred Ivey – both)*

These two photographs taken in July 1964 depict trains at or near Adelaide. **Above:** The 11.20 am from Great Victoria St to Londonderry (Foyle Road) enters Adelaide station behind UTA S class 4-4-0 No.60, *Slieve Donard*, (formerly GNR(I) No.172). **Right:** This scene, farther down the line on the approach to Adelaide station, features a cross-border service composed of CIE stock, the 10.30 am from Great Victoria St to Dublin (Amiens St). The train is hauled by 141 class diesel No.B166, one of thirty-seven such machines built in 1962 by General Motors at Illinois, USA. *(Marcus Eavis/Online Transport Archive – both)*

Leaving Belfast, we now proceed in a vaguely anti-clockwise direction around Northern Ireland, starting with the former Belfast & County Down Railway (BCDR) line from Belfast to Bangor. This twelve mile branch is the last remaining part of the BCDR's eighty mile network of railways in Co Down. The company operated for 100 years until it was absorbed into the newly created nationalised body, the UTA, on 1 October 1948. This view shows NCC MED power car No.30, part of a six-coach set, leaving Holywood and skirting Belfast Lough on its way to Bangor on 19 October 1957. In the foreground is a BCDR trespass notice. One of the stations on the line is Cultra, home of the Ulster Folk and Transport Museum. Its railway collection includes the only BCDR steam locomotive, Type 20 4-4-2 No.30 (later UTA No.230), built by Beyer, Peacock in 1901. *(W.E. Robertson/Online Transport Archive)*

Pictured at York Road depot on 9 June 1957 is ex-BCDR six-wheeled coach No.160. The vehicle is painted in UTA brunswick green livery, which replaced BCDR's crimson lake. Five BCDR carriages, including six-wheeler No.154, have been preserved by the Downpatrick & County Down Railway. This heritage railway currently operates over part of the former BCDR from its base at Downpatrick, located on the main line from Belfast (Queen's Quay) to Newcastle that closed in 1950. The railway proposes to extend beyond its current three mile limit to reach Ballydugan. *(Paul de Beer/Online Transport Archive)*

NCC steam would probably have become extinct by 1966 had it not been for two factors. The first was the need to overhaul the unreliable diesel railcar fleet, allowing some steam substitution on passenger services. More significant, however, was the awarding of an initial contract to the railway lasting from 1966 to 1970 for the transportation of spoil for a motorway construction project. WT class 2-6-4 tanks, nicknamed 'Jeeps', were used and this view shows No.53 at the head of one of these spoil trains leaving Magheramourne quarry on 20 August 1969. A huge heap of spoil had accumulated there, being the residue from the cement works and limestone quarry, and further quantities were removed under a further contract in the 1970s using diesel traction hauling the same wagons. *(Jerome McWatt/Online Transport Archive)*

These special freight trains operated on the Belfast–Larne line. Having delivered spoil to Greencastle, a suburb of Belfast, where the motorway was being built on reclaimed land on the edge of Belfast Lough, Jeep No.55 pushes a train of empty spoil wagons towards Carrickfergus, and onwards to Magheramourne on 19 August 1969. Seventy of these wagons were specially built for Northern Ireland by Cravens of Sheffield, twenty of which normally formed a train with a Jeep locomotive at each end. Members of the class of eighteen that were in the best condition worked these trains and were fitted with enlarged bunkers to minimise the need to replenish supplies of coal.
(Jerome McWatt/Online Transport Archive)

These two pictures dating from 28 April 1969 were taken at Whitehead, Co Antrim, best known nowadays to railway enthusiasts as the principal home of the RPSI. **Above:** Viewed through the windscreen of a passing diesel unit, Jeep No.56, with No.51 at the rear, heads south with a loaded spoil train. **Right:** No.10 skirts the western side of Belfast Lough, heading southwards with another loaded spoil train. The last of these trains ran on 2 May 1970, making the Jeeps the final steam locomotives to run in normal mainline service anywhere in the British Isles. Indeed, it was only just over a month earlier that one had hauled the last steam passenger service on Northern Ireland Railways (NIR). *(Bernard Harrison – both)*

The Belfast to Larne line, featured in this photograph, belonged to the Belfast & Northern Counties Railway (BNCR) until this company was acquired by the Midland Railway (Northern Counties Committee) in 1903. As stated previously, the NCC was taken over by the UTA in 1948, which was in turn absorbed into Northern Ireland Railways (NIR) in 1968. On 28 April 1969, a passenger service is seen near Greenisland, about to pass one of the BNCR's characteristic somersault signals. The leading vehicle, now carrying NIR livery, is ex-UTA Multi-Purpose Diesel (MPD) single-cab power car No.51. Greenisland is situated in Co Antrim on the edge of Belfast Lough, some seven miles from the capital. *(Bernard Harrison)*

A little to the south-west of Belfast but within the Belfast Metropolitan Area is Lisburn. The railway station was opened in 1839 by the Ulster Railway, which became one of the three railway companies that were combined into the newly formed GNR(I) in 1876. This company then rebuilt the station in 1878 but by the time this photograph was taken on 2 July 1964, it had been taken over by UTA following the demise of the GNR Board in 1958. The disreputable-looking locomotive in this scene is ex-GNR(I) S class 4-4-0 No.174, *Carrantuohill*, which has lost its nameplate and is showing little evidence of its lined blue livery. This was one of three S class locos acquired by CIE from the GNR Board in 1958 and then sold to UTA in June 1963. *(Paul de Beer/Online Transport Archive)*

This is how UTA's Antrim station appeared on 19 June 1955. Surprisingly, it looks much the same today, even retaining the delightful waiting room on the up platform, but the footbridge was replaced in 2001. W class 2-6-0 No.93, *The Foyle*, steams in from Londonderry on its way to Belfast. The station was opened in 1848 by the Belfast & Ballymena Railway, which became the Belfast & Northern Counties Railway (BNCR) in 1860, and the present buildings date from 1901-02, designed by Berkeley Deane Wise. From 1871, the GNR(I) had an adjacent station serving its branch to Lisburn but it closed in 1960 and the line is currently mothballed. *(Neil Davenport – all)*

Portrush station on the Co Antrim coast is the terminus of a short branch from Coleraine, Co Londonderry. The line opened in 1855 and in 1893 the station buildings were rebuilt in mock-Tudor style designed by the BNCR's engineer and architect, B.D. Wise. These buildings survive today, including the clock tower visible here, and have been adapted for retail use. A minimalist station now exists with only one platform in regular use. This photograph taken shortly after NIR replaced UTA in 1968 depicts a three-car multi-engined diesel unit (MED) with power car No.9 ahead of a former steam-stock trailer. Standing alongside is one of the Jeep 2-6-4 tanks which were drafted in about this period for some passenger services due to the unreliability of the aged MED and MPD units, requiring a major diesel repair programme to be undertaken. The first MED had entered service back in 1952 and the last was not withdrawn until 1978. *(Jerome McWatt/Online Transport Archive)*

This Park Royal-bodied AEC Regal IV, No.271 in the GNR Board's bus fleet, was one of thirty-three such vehicles that entered service between 1954 and 1956 and became the Board's last new buses. The entire road fleet was transferred to CIE upon the Board's dissolution in 1958 and No.271, which dated from October 1954, was withdrawn in 1972. It was in fact the only one of the thirty-three to have been registered in Belfast, the rest of the fleet bearing Dublin or Dundalk registrations. The bus is pictured in July 1957 outside the GNR(I)'s station in Foyle Street, Londonderry, which closed on 15 February 1965 when services on the line to Portadown via Omagh (the 'Derry Road') were withdrawn. Londonderry used to have four stations served by four different companies: two narrow gauge (the Londonderry & Lough Swilly and County Donegal, the latter being the operator on behalf of NCC) and two standard gauge (belonging to the GNR(I) and NCC). These last two competing lines survived into the 1960s but the Benson Report of 1963 recommended the closure of both, which would have left Londonderry 'rail-less'. However, the NCC's ex-BNCR route from Belfast via Coleraine was reprieved. *(Peter Grace)*

Strabane, Co Tyrone, used to be a busy railway junction on the Irish border where the standard-gauge GNR(I) met the narrow-gauge lines of the County Donegal Railway Joint Committee (CDRJC). The latter closed on 1 January 1960 (apart from freight between Strabane and Stranorlar that lasted until 6 February 1960), leaving the standard-gauge part of the station that closed on 15 February 1965. **Above:** UTA U class 4-4-0 No.66 (formerly GNR(I) No.201, *Meath*) brings freight into Strabane in July 1964. **Right upper:** The joint station, showing the CDRJC platforms on the left with two diesel railcars and standard-gauge tracks on the right. In the foreground is a mixed-gauge wagon turntable used when narrow-gauge bodies were winched onto standard-gauge wagons, and vice versa. **Right lower:** The nameboard as seen on 10 June 1957, similar to one preserved at Cultra. *(Marcus Eavis, Harry Luff, Paul de Beer/Online Transport Archive)*

The following sequence of photographs depicts the CDRJC 3ft narrow-gauge railway, starting with a view at Strabane in 1958 of railcar No.20, built by Walker Bros of Wigan in 1950. Along with No.19, these were the most modern railcars on the CDRJC and when the railway closed both were bought for use on the Isle of Man railways. There they had to operate back to back due to having only one driving cab and the absence of turntables. Following regular use in the early years of their transfer, both have latterly been partially restored but work on them is currently suspended. On the CDRJC, railcars operating mixed trains normally only hauled light goods vehicles, designated by their red livery, but No.20 appears to be additionally attached to a heavier van, these being painted grey. *(J.L. Stevenson)*

The CDRJC pioneered the use of railcars for passenger services, introducing the first as early as 1930 (making it unique in the British Isles at that time), but retained a sizeable steam fleet up to the end, used mainly on freight trains and heavy excursion or mixed trains. This view at Strabane shed in 1953 depicts class 5 2-6-4 tank No.8 *Foyle*, built by Nasmyth, Wilson & Co, Patricroft, Manchester, in 1908. Originally No.19, *Raphoe*, it was renumbered and renamed in 1937 and scrapped in 1955. The CDRJC had eight class 5 and 5A 2-6-4 tanks, four of which survive today, these being No.2, No.4, No.5 and No.6. *(W.E. Robertson/Online Transport Archive)*

This view at Strabane in 1957 of a shunting operation features one of the CDRJC's four class 4 Baltic 4-6-4 tanks and the only one to survive until the railway's closure. No.14, *Erne,* was another Nasmyth, Wilson & Co product, built in 1904, and was almost preserved, having been earmarked for export to the USA. When this scheme fell through it was sadly scrapped in 1968. The CDRJC section of Strabane station provided routes to Londonderry, Letterkenny, Stranorlar, Glenties and Donegal and, combined with the GNR(I)'s lines, Strabane was Ireland's busiest railway junction in the first half of the twentieth century. It was also a British Customs post for rail travellers entering Northern Ireland from the Republic. *(W.E. Robertson/Online Transport Archive)*

There is more shunting taking place at Strabane, this time on 12 September 1959 using CDRJC No.11, *Phoenix*, an appropriate name for this strange machine. Built in 1928 by Atkinson-Walker of Preston as a geared steam tractor for the Clogher Valley Railway (CVR) in Co Tyrone/Co Fermanagh, becoming No.8 on that railway, it proved unsuccessful and in 1932 was bought by the CDRJC whose general manager at the time, Henry Forbes, was on the CVR management committee. Forbes had the steam boiler removed, which was then sold to a local laundry, and the machine was rebuilt and fitted with a Gardner diesel engine. The contraption lasted until the railway's closure and is now preserved at Cultra.
(J.L. Stevenson)

The first station out of Strabane on the Letterkenny line was Lifford, Co Donegal, where there was an Irish Customs post for rail travellers entering the Republic from Strabane. Like all cross-border railway companies, the CDRJC suffered from the inconvenience and service delays arising from the partition of Ireland, which necessitated Customs border checks. In this view from May 1957, class 5 2-6-4 tank No.6, *Columbkille*, built by Nasmyth, Wilson & Co in 1907, pulls out of Lifford station hauling a long mixed train. This locomotive is now in the custody of the Foyle Valley Railway at its currently closed museum at the former GNR(I) Foyle Road station in Derry. *(Bruce Jenkins)*

No.2, *Blanche*, receives attention over the pit at Letterkenny shed in July 1959. This class 5A 2-6-4 tank, now preserved at Cultra, was built by Nasmyth, Wilson & Co in 1912 and was originally No.2A, signifying a duplicate number because the 2-6-4 replaced the original No.2, *Blanche*, which was a 2-4-0 tank. The name relates to a member of Lord Lifford's family, this peer being the one-time chairman of the CDR Joint Board. The Donegal Railway Company, which resulted from the merger of the West Donegal Light Railway and the Finn Valley Railway in 1892, had experienced financial difficulties in the early 1900s, resulting in its purchase in 1906 by the GNR(I) and England's Midland Railway (Northern Counties Committee), with the consequent creation of the CDR Joint Board. *(Bruce Jenkins)*

These two photographs were taken in the shed yard at Letterkenny. **Above:** Class 5A 2-6-4 tank No.1, *Alice* (originally No.21 *Ballyshannon* when built in 1912 until 1928), shows off its bright geranium-red livery with single thin yellow lining on 15 October 1953. **Right:** In faded red livery, class 5 2-6-4 tank No.6, *Columbkille* (previously No.18, *Killybegs*, from 1907-1937), rests between duties in July 1957. As stated on page 52, this 2-6-4 tank is located at the closed Foyle Valley Railway museum, where No.4 (*see page 57*) also exists. *(Paul de Beer/Online Transport Archive; Peter Grace)*

Railcar No.14, built in 1935, stands at Letterkenny station in July 1957. The bodies of these railcars were built by the GNR(I) at Dundalk and the driving units by Walker Bros of Wigan. Power was provided by a Gardner 6L2 diesel engine. The branch from Strabane to Letterkenny opened in January 1909, by which time the Joint Board was in control and both the GNR(I) and the NCC provided finance for the construction of the line. The County Donegal railways had been built in various stages from 1863 and the Letterkenny branch was the final section, bringing the total CDRJC mileage close to 125 miles. *(Peter Grace)*

The distinctive pinnacle on the left of this photograph belongs to Stranorlar station in Co Donegal, where the line from Strabane split, with one branch to Glenties and the other to Donegal. The Glenties line closed in 1947 to passengers and 1952 to freight but some two miles of the line alongside Lough Finn has been restored by the heritage Fintown Railway, with services operated by Walker Railcar No.18. Seen in this picture working a freight is class 5 2-6-4 tank No.4, *Meenglas* (No.16, *Donegal*, from entry into service in 1907 until 1937). The locomotive exists at the Foyle Valley Railway museum at Derry. The survival of so many ex-CDRJB assets is largely due to an aborted scheme to export them to the USA by Dr Ralph Cox of New Jersey. The items were stored at various CDRJB locations for several years but were then disposed of when the proposed export failed. *(Bruce Jenkins)*

Left: One of the pair of CDRJC's most modern diesel railcars (No.19 and No.20), built by the GNR(I)/Walker Bros in 1950 is seen at Lough Eske, on the Donegal branch, on 16 June 1955. **Above:** Railcar No.16 shunts lightweight and heavier vans at Donegal on 8 March 1958. The eighteen mile Stranorlar–Donegal line, built to 3ft narrow gauge by the West Donegal Railway, opened in 1889. However, the line from Strabane to Stranorlar, opened by the Finn Valley Railway in 1863, was standard gauge (5ft 3ins). When the two railways merged to form the Donegal Railway Company in 1892, the standard-gauge section was relaid to narrow gauge. *(Neil Davenport (page 58 – both); Paul de Beer/Online Transport Archive)*

Bypassing Omagh, Fintona Junction and Bundoran Junction for the moment, we move to the border town of Enniskillen, Co Fermanagh, Northern Ireland. The GNR(I)'s engine shed is a hive of activity on 11 June 1957 with a pair of 4-4-0s raring to go. Yet, just over three months later, on 1 October 1957, the Northern Ireland Government closed most of the GNR(I) north of the border including the main line through Enniskillen from Omagh to Dundalk in the Republic. The locomotive nearest the camera is PP class No.44, named *Leinster* for the first three years of its life from 1911-14. On the disbanding of the GNR Board in 1958 it was transferred to CIE and withdrawn two years later. The rails beside the depot led south to Dundalk and to the right are the lines of the Sligo, Leitrim and Northern Counties Railway (SLNCR), which also ran into Enniskillen. The brick building on the platform was the company's headquarters. *(Paul de Beer/Online Transport Archive)*

GNR(I) AL class 0-6-0 No.59, originally built by Beyer, Peacock in 1893 and named *Kilkenny* until 1913, shunts coal trucks in Enniskillen depot yard opposite the station. The tracks in the foreground were used by SLNCR trains, which terminated at Enniskillen. This was the eastern end of the line to Sligo, in the Republic, which was nearly fifty miles in length and traversed four counties: Fermanagh, Cavan (just!), Leitrim and Sligo. The SLNCR closed on the same day as this part of the GNR(I) because the railway served sparse areas in the west of Ireland and was not viable without access to the GNR(I) junction at Enniskillen and points eastwards. Turn to the next page to find the occupant of the platform track nearest the camera. *(Paul de Beer/Online Transport Archive)*

Above: SLNCR Railcar B stands in the bay at Enniskillen, with the 1859-built main station building in the background. This fifty-nine-seater vehicle was built by Walker Bros of Wigan in 1947 and, following closure of the SLNCR, became CIE's railcar No.2509. It is currently awaiting restoration on the heritage Downpatrick & County Down Railway. **Upper right:** Contrasting dramatically with the modern appearance of Railcar B, SLNCR Railbus 2A, coupled to a luggage van, has just left Enniskillen having travelled across Weir's Bridge over the River Erne (visible behind the vehicle). **Lower right:** One of three bogie coaches built for the SLNCR by Hurst Nelson of Motherwell in 1924.
(Paul de Beer/Online Transport Archive – all)

Here is a close-up of Railbus 2A in June 1957 standing in the bay platform at Enniskillen, again coupled to a luggage van. This petrol-powered road bus comprised a Leyland PLSC Lion chassis with a Gardner 6LW engine and GNR(I)-built body. It was supplied to the SLNCR by the GNR(I) in 1938. Originally it was fitted with pneumatic-tyred railway wheels but these caused problems with electric circuits for signalling and were later replaced with rail wheels. Notice how the sun has highlighted the railbus' starting handle! To the right of the vehicle is GNR(I) U class 4-4-0 No.203, *Armagh*, built by Beyer, Peacock in 1948 and withdrawn by CIE in November 1962. (*Nick Nicolson/The Transport Treasury*)

SLNCR 0-6-4 tank *Lough Melvin* takes water at Manorhamilton, Co Leitrim, on 8 June 1957. This was one of two locomotives built for the SLNCR in 1949 by Beyer, Peacock. Both were bought by UTA in 1959 for shunting, replacing older engines, and this one became No.26 (the SLNCR did not number its engines, identifying them by name only). No.26 was withdrawn in 1965 but its twin (No.27, *Lough Erne*) has been preserved (*see page 24*). Manorhamilton was approximately halfway between Enniskillen and Sligo and was the location of the company's main workshops. *(Nick Nicolson/The Transport Treasury)*

This is another view of the SLNCR at Manorhamilton on 8 June 1957, with 0-6-4 tank *Lough Melvin* in the distance on the extreme left. In the centre is Hurst Nelson composite bogie coach No.10 and on the right is one of five Beyer, Peacock 0-6-4 tanks of the Leitrim class. This example, *Lissadell*, was built in 1899, and sold in 1954 to the Hammond Lane Foundry. The locomotive returned to Manorhamilton to be broken up soon after this picture was taken. Lissadell itself is a mansion in Co Sligo and was the ancestral home of Countess Markievicz (née Constance Gore-Booth) who in 1918 became the first woman to be elected to the House of Commons, although, as a leading Irish Republican, she refused to take her seat at Westminster. *(Nick Nicolson/The Transport Treasury)*

Returning northwards, Bundoran Junction, near Kilskeery, Co Tyrone, was the point where trains for the branch to the seaside resort of Bundoran, Co Donegal, in the Republic diverged from those going from Omagh to Enniskillen and beyond. Both lines were built by separate independent railway companies and were absorbed by the GNR(I) in 1883. This photograph, looking towards Omagh, was taken from the road bridge over the station on 8 June 1957, and features GNR(I) PP class 4-4-0 No.50, named *Donard* until 1914, a Beyer, Peacock product from 1911. This engine became UTA 50X in 1958 and was withdrawn in March 1960. The station closed on 1 October 1957 but much of it still remains to this day and Bundoran Junction North signal cabin, visible in the distance, has been preserved at the heritage Downpatrick and County Down Railway. *(Nick Nicolson/The Transport Treasury)*

Heading back towards Omagh brings us to Fintona Junction, Co Tyrone, and the GNR(I)'s remarkable standard-gauge horse tram, seen here on 8 June 1957 after the animal had been turned for the journey back to Fintona. In front of the signal cabin a small shed can be seen. This was where the horse was put in between duty to reduce the risk of it being frightened by a steam engine entering the station and stampeding with the car (or 'van', as it was called by locals). The horse was always known as 'Dick', regardless of gender. *(Nick Nicolson/The Transport Treasury)*

The horse tram service to Fintona, Co Tyrone, opened in 1853 and became part of the GNR(I) in 1883. From that date, conveyance was by GNR(I) No.381, a tramcar built in that year by the Metropolitan Railway Carriage & Wagon Company, Saltley, Birmingham, with upstairs 'knifeboard' (central back to back) seating. The service closed on 1 October 1957, along with much of the GNR(I) including Fintona Junction, and the tramcar is now preserved at Cultra. In July 1957, 'Dick' is pictured leaving Fintona on the fifteen-minute slightly uphill journey to the Junction. *(Peter Grace)*

A CIE train bound for Dublin (Amiens Street) stands in Omagh station, Co Tyrone, in July 1964. Omagh was the junction for the GNR(I) lines to Enniskillen and Portadown. The rusty track on the left led to Enniskillen, which closed on 1 October 1957, and the track on which the train is standing was the so-called 'Derry Road'. This latter track controversially closed on 15 February 1965 because it duplicated the former BNCR Belfast to Londonderry line via Coleraine that was faster, due to its being some five miles shorter and having easier gradients. The locomotive is one of the thirty-seven Bo-Bo diesel electrics of the 141 class built by General Motors of Illinois, USA, which entered service from December 1962 and have proved most successful. Their predicted lifespan of forty years has been exceeded by more than ten years and several have been preserved. *(Marcus Eavis/Online Transport Archive)*

Omagh had extensive freight facilities, occupying a number of stone buildings, one of which is in use today as a tyre service retailer in James Street. This, and another stone building, are all that remain of the railway at Omagh, the station having already been demolished. The locomotive seen here is UTA No.43, a Beyer, Peacock SG class 0-6-0, formerly GNR(I) No.17, dating from 1913 and withdrawn in May 1965. Behind the engine is the optical illusion of a UTA bus perched precariously on top of a slag heap! *(Marcus Eavis/Online Transport Archive)*

The next main station eastwards from Omagh to Portadown on the GNR(I)'s 'Derry Road' was Dungannon, Co Tyrone, seen here in August 1964. **Above:** Facing eastwards towards Portadown is a two-coach local train with van attached, headed by UTA No.48. This UG class 0-6-0 was built by Beyer, Peacock in 1948, becoming GNR(I) No.146, and was withdrawn in June 1967. The footbridge roof has been removed but the supports remain. **Opposite:** Former NCC W class 2-6-0 No.91, *The Bush* (named after a river in Co Antrim), approaches Dungannon station with a westbound freight. This locomotive was one of eight such moguls transferred to work on the former GNR(I) lines taken over by the UTA in 1958, but they soon ended up in poor condition as a result of working heavy freight trains over this hilly route. *(Roy Hobbs – both)*

Taken in June 1957, this photograph of Dungannon station shows the footbridge when it still had its roof intact. Also visible is a GNR(I) clerestory-roofed vehicle and, facing the camera (and Portadown), GNR(I) Q class 4-4-0 No.130, named *Saturn* until 1914. Built by Neilson Reid in 1901, this veteran passed to CIE in 1958 and was withdrawn in October 1959. There were thirteen members of the class, all built between 1899 and 1904, and one (No.131) has been preserved (*see pages 13 and 88*). (*Nick Nicolson/The Transport Treasury*)

We have now reached Portadown where the station is still open, serving the Belfast–Dublin main line and the Bangor branch, but without the imposing building with Italianate portico at the top of Watson Street pictured here in July 1964. This was demolished and replaced in 1970 by a functional, more modest structure befitting the station's reduced importance as a railway junction following the closure of the GNR(I) line to Cavan in the Republic via Armagh and Clones in 1957 and the 'Derry Road' in 1965. Only the two entry pillars to the forecourt survive, between which a mural depicting the old station has recently been installed. *(Marcus Eavis/Online Transport Archive)*

Entering Portadown from the north in August 1962 is UTA S2 class 4-4-0 No.62, formerly GNR(I) No.190, *Lugnaquilla*, a Beyer, Peacock machine originating in 1915 and lasting in service until 1965, following its transfer to UTA in 1958. Only three S2 locomotives were built, although visually they strongly resembled the five S class engines such as the preserved No.171, *Slieve Gullion*. The S2s arrived just too late to receive the GNR(I)'s locomotive green livery, which was applied from 1881 to 1913, and were therefore among the first to be painted black. Sky-blue livery was not introduced until 1936. *(Fred Ivey)*

Another UTA W class mogul to be transferred to work on former GNR(I) lines was No.99, *King George VI*, seen here at Portadown station on 10 May 1962. The W class of 2-6-0s was basically a tender version of the LMS Fowler 2-6-4 tanks and the first four were built at Derby, with the remainder, including No.99, being built by the NCC at York Road Works, Belfast. The engine was delivered in May 1938 and was withdrawn in October 1964. This was the last full year in which any of the moguls worked and it is tragic that none has survived, despite the fact that the scrapping of No.97, *Earl of Ulster,* was deferred for six months, possibly with preservation in mind. *(Jim Oatway)*

The various classes of 0-6-0s belonging to the UTA, CIE and GNR(I) were an indispensable part of steam operation across Ireland and, although primarily designed for freight, were often used on passenger trains and could be regarded as being mixed traffic. However, the GNR(I) SG3 class of fifteen 0-6-0s were specifically designed as heavy goods engines, given a power classification of 'D' and nicknamed 'Big Ds'. The one seen here outside Portadown shed on 10 May 1962, UTA No.37 (ex-GNR(I) No.97), was built by Beyer, Peacock in 1921. Although this engine was withdrawn in December 1965, it was not cut up until 1969, so it could in theory have been preserved but, as with the last W class mogul, there was sadly not enough money. *(Jim Oatway)*

UTA SG2 class 0-6-0 No.40 (ex-GNR(I) No.18 dating from 1924) stands on the turntable at Portadown depot on 10 May 1962. In the background are W class mogul No.94, *The Maine*, and SG3 class 0-6-0 No.32 (ex-GNR(I) No.13). The GNR(I) built this distinctive pre-cast concrete, twelve-track semi-roundhouse in 1926, together with an identical one at Clones, Co Monaghan. The one at Portadown was located at Portadown Junction between the lines to Dublin and Clones. It closed in November 1965 and the remaining steam inhabitants transferred to Adelaide Shed. The concrete structure at Portadown was demolished by the British Army using explosives but the one at Clones survives today within an industrial complex. *(Jim Oatway)*

Still at Portadown on 10 May 1962 and representing another 0-6-0 type operated by UTA, UG class 0-6-0 No.48 is shunting in the yard. This locomotive was previously GNR(I) No.146, a Beyer, Peacock product dating from 1948 that survived until 1968. There were ten members of the class, with five being built in 1937 and a further five in 1948; they were regarded as light mixed traffic engines, often being used on local passenger and excursion workings. *(Jim Oatway)*

Travelling south on the GNR(I) from Portadown towards the border, we reach Goraghwood where passengers to Northern Ireland were subject to Customs checks and consequent delays. This picture taken in June 1957 depicts GNR(I) V class 4-4-0 No.85, *Merlin* (since preserved), one of five such three-cylinder compounds, all built by Beyer, Peacock in 1932 (but not the tenders that were constructed at the GNR(I)'s Dundalk Works). The V class was designed to haul accelerated Dublin–Belfast expresses but were largely displaced on these duties by the post-war VS class 4-4-0s. *(Nick Nicolson/The Transport Treasury)*

Here is a shot of another UG class 0-6-0, this time UTA No.47, formerly GNR(I) No.82. The locomotive was one of the earlier class members, differing slightly from the post-war Beyer, Peacock batch, and was built by the GNR(I) at its Dundalk Works in 1937. It is seen at Newry (Edward Street) working the 9.30 am freight to Portadown. This station was on the branch to Warrenpoint and closed on 4 January 1965. Although there is currently a station called Newry, this one is some three miles from the town centre and opened in 1984. It is situated on the Belfast–Dublin main line at Bessbrook, whose station originally closed in 1942. *(Ernie's Railway Archive)*

Warrenpoint, Co Down, is a coastal resort in a scenic setting on the northern shore of Carlingford Lough. The six mile branch from Newry to Warrenpoint opened in 1849 and was intended to continue to Rostrevor, but this never happened. The station at Warrenpoint was rebuilt by the GNR(I) in 1891 and closed on 4 January 1965 despite the heavy amount of excursion rail traffic bringing tourists to enjoy the resort and to take the short ferry journey across the Lough to Omeath, Co Louth, in the Republic. In this picture dating from August 1962, UTA S class 4-4-0 No.60, *Slieve Donard*, formerly GNR(I) No.172 built by Beyer, Peacock in 1913, backs a rake of passenger stock into Warrenpoint station, which includes a carriage still carrying GNR(I) grained mahogany livery. *(Fred Ivey)*

There is plenty of activity at Warrenpoint station in these views in August 1962. **Left:** Two 4-4-0s, S class UTA No.60, *Slieve Donard* (ex-GNR(I) No.172), and S2 class UTA No.63, *Slievenamon* (ex-GNR(I) No.192), flank UTA SG2 class 0-6-0 No.38, formerly GNR(I) No.16. **Above:** No.38 prepares to leave with a train containing two ex-GNR(I) carriages in mahogany livery. Unusually for an ex-GNR(I) locomotive, No.38 was not built by Beyer, Peacock or by the GNR(I) but by Nasmyth Wilson & Co, Salford, Manchester, one of five constructed in 1924-25. *(Fred Ivey – both)*

Continuing our journey on the eastern side of Ireland, we now cross the border into Co Louth, arriving at Dundalk, halfway between the capital cities of Belfast and Dublin and appropriately chosen by the GNR(I) as the location of its railway works. Consequently, it is fitting to find there an ex-GNR(I) locomotive, now owned by CIE, still looking smart in its former owner's sky-blue livery in July 1959. The engine is S class 4-4-0 No.170, *Errigal* (CIE did not renumber the acquired locomotives), built by Beyer, Peacock in 1913. Three members of the S class were sold to UTA in June 1963, including this one, and all were withdrawn in December 1965. *(Donald Nevin)*

UTA trains also crossed the border into Dundalk, with a certain number continuing to travel along the former GNR(I) main line all the way to Dublin. These trains were sometimes even hauled by Jeep tanks, although an experiment after CIE had withdrawn steam operation in 1963 that involved attaching an auxiliary tender filled with coal and water (the Republic was short of coal) proved unsuccessful. This picture depicts a Belfast–Dundalk semi-fast at Dundalk in July 1959 hauled by Jeep No.51 built at Derby in 1949. This locomotive was the penultimate member of the WT class to remain in service, lasting until October 1970, but was scrapped in the following February. *(Donald Nevin)*

This scene at Dundalk shed in August 1962 is remarkable because it depicts two extant locomotives that have been running in Ireland in the preservation era. On the left is S class 4-4-0 No.171, *Slieve Gullion*. This engine was built by Beyer, Peacock and delivered to the GNR(I) in 1913, going on to be acquired by CIE in 1958 and sold to UTA in June 1963. It was withdrawn in December 1965 and bought by the RPSI in the following month. On the right is a locomotive depicted earlier, Q class mixed traffic 4-4-0 No.131, *Uranus* (name removed in 1914), built by Neilson Reid in Glasgow and delivered to the GNR(I) in 1901. Acquired by CIE in 1958, it was withdrawn in October 1963 and was steamed by the RPSI for the first time in more than fifty years in 2015. *(Fred Ivey)*

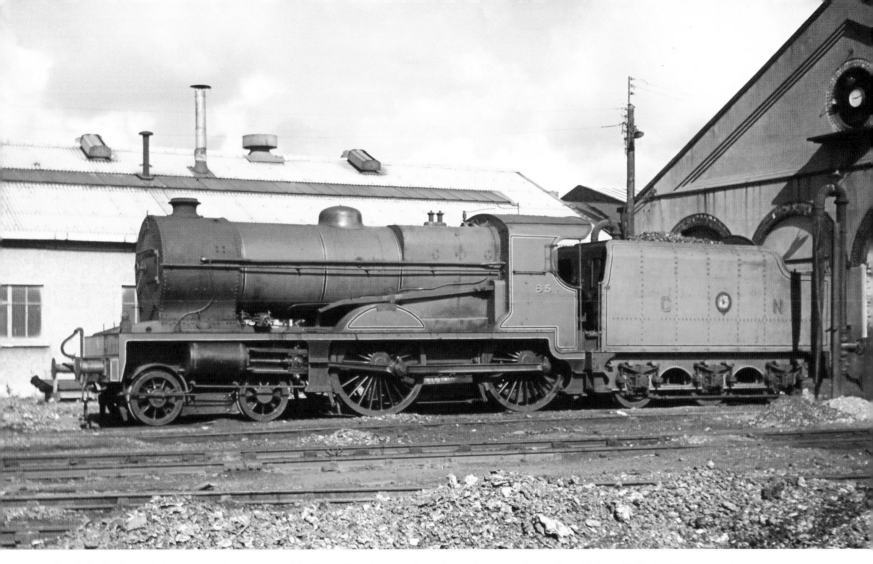

Dundalk shed certainly seems to have attracted lucky engines because here is another one, pictured on 16 June 1962. Looking somewhat grubbier than it did on page 81, this is GNR(I) V class 4-4-0 No.85, *Merlin*, again. Passing to CIE in 1958, No.85 is the only V class engine to survive and, following its withdrawal in 1965, belongs to the Ulster Folk & Transport Museum at Cultra, but is leased to the RPSI, who own the tender, and is currently main-line operational. *(J.L. Stevenson)*

The most modern diesel trains ordered by the GNR(I) before its demise were sixteen power cars with small cabs (Nos.701-716) and eight (Nos.901-908) with full-width cabs. Fitted with powerful 11.3 litre engines, they were known as the BUT railcars, BUT (British United Traction) being an AEC/Leyland specialist joint venture company formed in 1946. The new railcars were designed to run with intermediate carriages adapted from former steam stock and the first units entered service on the cross-border Enterprise service (*see page 108*) in June 1957. The initial train consisted of a six-coach set including three power cars. This picture at Dundalk was also taken in June 1957 and depicts newly delivered 701 series power cars carrying Enterprise Express markings. *(Nick Nicolson/The Transport Treasury)*

From the GNR(I)'s most modern railcars we now turn to one of its oldest and strangest looking, photographed at Dundalk at the same time. This is articulated railcar C1 viewed from the rear. With only one driving compartment (here seen at the other end), it suffered from the disadvantage of needing a turntable when it reached a terminus. Also, it lacked conventional buffers, although it could haul a small luggage trailer. Railcar C, its original designation until 1935, was the GNR(I)'s third diesel railcar and was completed in November 1934 at Dundalk Works. For much of its early life it was used on services between Enniskillen and Bundoran and CIE operated it for a time after acquiring it in 1958, until it was withdrawn in September 1961. *(Nick Nicolson/The Transport Treasury)*

The next large town south of Dundalk on the GNR(I)'s main line to Dublin was Drogheda, where this photograph of a Belfast-bound train from Dublin with UTA stock was taken on the southern approaches to the station on 11 May 1962. The locomotive is CIE A class (later 001 class) No.A43, one of sixty built by Metropolitan-Vickers in Manchester in 1955-56, which were the mainstay of mainline trains through to the 1990s. However, their longevity owed nothing to the original Crossley engines, which proved so unreliable that they were replaced by General Motors EMD engines between 1968 and 1971. The last of the class was withdrawn in 1995 and four have been preserved. *(Jim Oatway)*

The same loaded barrow that can be seen in the previous picture indicates that we are still at the southern end of Drogheda station on 11 May 1962, but this time looking north. Puffing past the signal box is ex-GNR(I) No. 44, becoming CIE No.164, an LQG class 0-6-0, originally named *Fintona*, built by North British in 1908 and withdrawn in November 1962. The tracks which the photographer is probably standing on were for Navan and Oldcastle (the line is still open to freight as far as Navan, which we will visit later). However, the signal box has been demolished, and most of the embankment and spruce trees have been cleared to make way for a diesel railcar depot. *(Jim Oatway)*

The lupins are blooming while GNR(I) railbus No.1 nestles in Oldcastle station, Co Meath, in June 1957. The branch from Drogheda to Navan was opened in 1850 and extended to Oldcastle, which became the terminus, in 1863. The GNR(I) took over the line in 1876 and it closed to passengers on 14 April 1958, with goods traffic being withdrawn on 1 April 1963. The section from Drogheda to just outside Navan, however, remains in use for Tara Mines traffic. Navan station still survives, as indeed does Oldcastle, complete with its train shed roof.
(Nick Nicolson/The Transport Treasury)

Clearly, there are no worries about the possibility of these children falling into the turntable pit as they take a ride on Railbus No.1 while it revolves at Oldcastle for the return journey to Drogheda! Return to page 15 for the history, and current location, of this fascinating vehicle. However, this picture provides an excellent view of the wheels, showing the Howden-Meredith rail wheel on the rear axle with pneumatic insert for a quieter ride (some railway companies in Great Britain had a similar idea using Mansell wooden inserts), whereas the pneumatics have been replaced on the front axle with railway wagon wheels. *(Nick Nicolson/The Transport Treasury)*

Approaching the northern outskirts of Dublin, the main line reaches Howth Junction, where the route to Sutton and Howth branches off to the peninsular, Howth now being the terminus of the Dublin Area Rapid Transit (DART) electric trains from Bray, south of Dublin. Up to 31 May 1959, Sutton, along with Howth, was an interchange with the GNR(I)'s Hill of Howth Tramway, acquired by CIE in 1958 following the dissolution of the GNR Board. This view, dating from 24 March 1957, depicts a Dublin–Howth service that outside peak hours would normally be operated by a diesel railcar. On this occasion, the train consists of compartment stock hauled by GNR(I) T2 class 4-4-2 tank No.62. This locomotive was built by Beyer, Peacock in 1929 and withdrawn in November 1960, following acquisition by CIE in 1958. *(Paul de Beer/Online Transport Archive)*

This is the tramway interchange at Sutton with car No.9, a seventy-three-seater built by Milnes of Shropshire in 1902, waiting to depart for Howth Summit in 1956. The tramway operated ten passenger-carrying trams but No.9 and No.10 were seldom used due to their larger size and also, until 1957 when replacement springs were fitted from withdrawn trams, their tendency to derail. With less exposure to damaging sea air, they retained the early grained mahogany livery, whereas Nos.1-8 were eventually repainted in the GNR(I)'s Oxford Blue and cream livery introduced in 1929, which was less prone to weathering. No.9 has been preserved at the National Transport Museum of Ireland at Howth and No.10, regauged from 5ft 3ins to 4ft 8^1/$_2$ins, is at the National Tramway Museum, Crich, Derbyshire. *(Paul de Beer/Online Transport Archive)*

These two pictures were taken in 1955 at Howth Summit, latterly known as Hill of Howth, which was 365 feet above sea level. **Left:** Car No.7 arrives from Sutton, photographed from the upper deck of another car subsequently seen, **Above**, descending the steep incline on its way to Howth while No.7 stands in the loop. Sutton and Howth stations were only two miles apart but when you took the scenic and windswept route by open-top tram, they were more than five miles apart! No.7 was one of the eight original sixty-seven-seater trams built for the line's opening in 1901 by Brush of Loughborough. It was scrapped when the line closed. *(Alex Hamilton/Leo Sullivan Collection – both)*

This is the interior of the tramcar depot at Sutton on 11 August 1958 and depicts, from left to right, car No.9 in grained mahogany livery; No.11, a tower wagon of doubtful origin; and No.4, now happily residing at Cultra. As previously mentioned, No.9 and No.10 are also preserved and to this list should be added No.2, which has been regauged for operation at the Orange Empire Railway Museum, Perris, California. Finally, although the body of No.6 was scrapped, its truck frames still exist, having been regauged and used for the restoration of Manchester Corporation Tramways No.765, which operates at Heaton Park in Manchester. *(Paul de Beer/Online Transport Archive)*

Connecting with the trams at Howth station on this sunny 1955 day is GNR(I)'s railcar F, watched by a girl perched on the sea wall as it arrives from Dublin. Built in March 1938, this articulated 164-seat unit consisted of a central engine section containing two Gardner 6LW diesel engines, with a passenger coach at each end. Railcar F was acquired by UTA in 1958 and, as UTA No.104, ended up on the Warrenpoint branch until withdrawal in November 1965. The GNR(I) signal box on the platform dates from the 1870s and was decommissioned in 1984 when the DART electrics reached Howth, but is still standing, albeit boarded up and fenced in. *(Alex Hamilton/Leo Sullivan Collection)*

At this point we move to Dublin, starting with Amiens Street station (now Dublin Connolly, renamed in 1966 along with fourteen other stations in the Republic to commemorate persons connected with Irish independence). This picture was taken on 26 March 1957 and depicts CIE 13 class 0-6-2 tank No.673 attached to an unpainted aluminium coach. This eye-catching livery, with red numerals, was introduced in late 1955 on new carriages to promote a modern image, but they soon looked tarnished and from 1958 were painted green to match older stock. No.673 belonged to a class of five such locomotives built for Great Southern Railways (GSR) in 1933-34 and used on commuter services between Dublin and Bray/ Greystones in Co Wicklow. Withdrawn in 1962, this engine outlived the other four by three years. *(Paul de Beer/Online Transport Archive)*

The GNR(I) ordered two 0-6-2 tanks from Robert Stephenson & Co in 1905 specifically for shunting duties. These were numbers 98 and 99 of class QGT, becoming class QGTs after being superheated in the 1930s. No.99, seen here at Amiens Street on 25 March 1957, outlived its twin by three years and was acquired by CIE in 1958, lasting in service until November 1960. There were a further two 0-6-2 shunting locomotives of this type, classified QGT2, built in 1911. Numbered 168 and 169, they were slightly larger and never superheated. Both were officially withdrawn in 1957 but had already been out of use for several years. *(Paul de Beer/Online Transport Archive)*

Building on its pre-war experience with diesel railbuses and railcars and in a further display of its progressive thinking, the GNR(I) possessed, by 1950-51, the largest fleet of diesel multiple units in the British Isles. These were formed from twenty Park Royal-bodied AEC power cars with 9.6 litre engines and pre-selector gearboxes, a description that could equally apply to a London Transport RT bus! With a power car at each end, these multiple units would normally run with one or two intermediate standard mainline carriages, all carrying the GNR(I)'s diesel livery of Oxford Blue and cream. In this photograph taken on 21 March 1959 railcar No.613 is bringing a multiple unit into Amiens Street station, with the locomotive depot visible in the background. Withdrawn in 1975, No.613 was owned by CIE when pictured here despite appearances suggesting GNR(I) days. *(Paul de Beer/Online Transport Archive)*

Having seen a train arrive at Amiens Street station, we now have one leaving. This is the 5.58 pm to Belfast (Great Victoria Street) in July 1964 hauled by ex-GNR(I) VS class 4-4-0 No.207, *Boyne*, built by Beyer, Peacock in 1948. This locomotive belonged to a class of five that were the last new 4-4-0s built anywhere in the world. One reason for the GNR(I) sticking to 4-4-0s for its express passenger trains was that nothing larger would fit into Dundalk Works! No.207 was acquired by CIE in 1958 and sold to UTA in June 1963. Being a late buy by UTA, it retained its GNR(I) number, unlike the other two acquired by UTA in 1958 that were renumbered. No.207 was withdrawn in December 1965, becoming the last survivor of the class, but it failed to be preserved. *(Marcus Eavis/Online Transport Archive)*

Against the backdrop of Amiens Street's large signal cabin in July 1959, ex-GNR(I) T2 class 4-4-2 tank No.67 takes a rest between station pilot duties. There were twenty such Glover superheated T2 tanks, all built between 1921 and 1930, making this the largest class on the GNR(I). These locomotives and their five un-superheated T1 class predecessors were the mainstay of GNR(I) suburban services in the Dublin and Belfast areas until the gradual arrival of diesel traction from the 1930s. Before 1948 No.67 had been No.147, at which point both it and No.149 had to surrender their numbers in favour of a new batch of UG class 0-6-0s to allow the latter to have sequential numbering. No.147, built by Beyer, Peacock in 1924, was acquired by CIE in 1958 and withdrawn in November 1960. *(Donald Nevin)*

Another picture taken in July 1959 at Amiens Street depicts a freight working hauled by CIE D2 class 4-4-0 No.322. This was originally a Great Southern & Western Railway (GSWR) engine constructed in 1905 at Inchicore Works, Dublin, and was substantially rebuilt in 1924, a year before the company was absorbed into the newly created GSR following the partition of Ireland. The locomotive was further modified in 1937 with the fitting of a superheated boiler. There were ultimately fourteen members in the class and initially these were the GSWR's principal express class until the 400 class 4-6-0s arrived in bulk in the early 1920s. No.322, along with No.329, were the last D2s in service, being withdrawn in 1960. Nos.324-6 were withdrawn as early as 1927-28! *(Donald Nevin)*

Through trains between Belfast and Dublin were normally delayed at Goraghwood in Northern Ireland and Dundalk in the Republic for Customs checks. However, in the face of airline and road competition, the GNR(I) overcame the problem from 11 August 1948 by running a non-stop service, the Enterprise Express, with Customs checks confined to the two termini: Great Victoria Street and Amiens Street. In May 1951, as seen here, the express was steam hauled but AEC diesel multiple units would soon take over the service and more modern diesel sets were introduced by the GNR Board in 1957 (see page 90). This view depicts VS class 4-4-0 No.206, Liffey, preparing to leave Amiens Street station. No.206 was the first of this class of five engines but achieved less than twelve years of service. (W.J. Wyse/LRTA collection)

Another picture from May 1951 depicts Inchicore running shed and centres on GSWR/GSR 400/B2 class 4-6-0 No.405, built by Armstrong Whitworth in 1923, one of nine class members built between 1921 and 1923, plus the doyen built in 1916. This was not a successful type of locomotive, although improvement in performance was obtained through two subsequent rebuilds, the first involving conversion from four to two cylinders. However, three were not converted and were withdrawn in 1929-30 after an extraordinarily short working life. No.405 was rebuilt with two cylinders in 1933 and rebuilt again in 1937 with a larger boiler. It was withdrawn in 1955. During their service life, the class was confined to the Dublin–Cork and Mallow–Killarney lines. *(WJ. Wyse/LRTA collection)*

We now visit Amiens Street shed on 11 May 1962 for a dramatic contrast in locomotive design! **Above:** This is the unfortunately named *Sambo*, allegedly built from spare parts in 1914 for use as the Inchicore Works shunter. It ended its life as the Amiens Street shunter in 1962 and has already lost its cab-side nameplate in this view. It never carried a number, although officially it was L2 class 0-4-2 saddletank No.842.

Right: B135 was one of fifteen such Bo-Bo diesels built by General Motors of Illinois, USA, and delivered to CIE in 1961 to replace steam on both passenger and freight duties. Two (No.124 and No.134) lasted until 2008 and have been preserved by the Irish Traction Group and RPSI respectively. The grey and yellow colours seen here were quickly replaced by the familiar black and tan livery. The locomotive shed building behind the diesel has returned to housing steam, being leased to the RPSI. *(Jim Oatway – both)*

Returning to Inchicore some three miles west of the city, the GSWR set up its main engineering works here in 1846 when the company opened its line from Dublin to Carlow, and Irish Rail continues using the works today. On 11 May 1962, former GNR(I) 0-6-0 crane tank No.31, built by Hawthorne Leslie in 1928 as the Dundalk Works shunter where it worked until 1960, had found its way to Inchicore. On the demise of the GNR Board in 1958, No.31 was handed over to the newly created Dundalk Engineering Works Ltd and was sold to CIE in 1960, making it their last steam acquisition. CIE allocated the locomotive to their departmental fleet, renumbering it 365A. The locomotive was broken up at Inchicore in 1965. *(Jim Oatway)*

Some two miles from Inchicore is Kingsbridge station (renamed Heuston in 1966), which was the Dublin terminus of the GSWR when the line to Carlow was opened in 1846. The station then went on to serve other towns in the south and west of Ireland including Waterford, Cork, Limerick and Galway. On 16 March 1959, GSWR/GSR 101/J15 class 0-6-0 No.122 was photographed shunting two carriages and six-wheeled Traffic Department Sleeping car No.224A, which had returned from Baltinglass (*see pages 121-122*). Locomotive No.122 was built at Inchicore in 1882 and modernised by the fitting of a superheated boiler and Belpaire firebox in 1942. It was withdrawn in 1963. *(Charles Firminger)*

In the north of Dublin stood Broadstone station (now a bus depot), the headquarters of the GSWR's competitor, the Midland Great Western Railway (MGWR), which built routes to Mullingar, Galway and Sligo, starting in 1847. In 1878, the MGWR constructed an engine shed and railway works (where engines were built) adjacent to Broadstone station. Passenger services were withdrawn from there in 1937, with trains diverted to Westland Row (renamed Dublin Pearse in 1966), and horse/cattle traffic was transferred to Liffey Junction. Broadstone shed closed on 8 April 1961 following the end of CIE steam in the Dublin area. This view dates from 16 March 1959. *(Charles Firminger)*

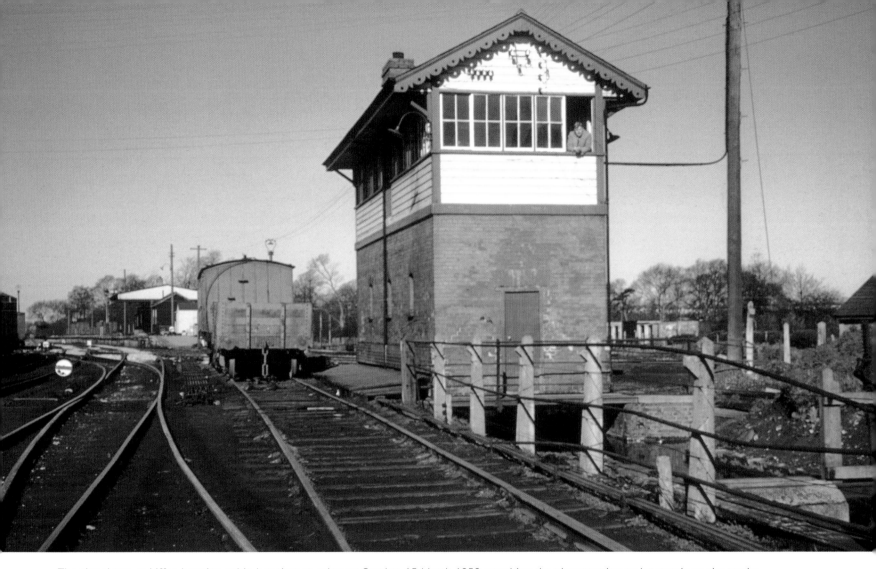

The signalman at Liffey Junction cabin has time to relax on Sunday, 15 March 1959, watching the photographer as he stands on the tracks (the shiny left-hand one comes from Broadstone shed). Liffey Junction station, visible in the background, opened in 1864 and closed on 18 January 1937 concurrent with the closure of Broadstone station. Liffey Junction was created when the Broadstone line met the subsequently built Dublin line to Amiens Street (now Connolly) and the North Wall yards. Commuter trains to Maynooth and long-distance trains to Sligo pass from right to left behind the box, which was ultimately set on fire by vandals and demolished following decommissioning in 1991. The trackbed of the lifted Broadstone line is now used for the LUAS Cross City tram line. *(Charles Firminger)*

Remaining in the Dublin area, this is a view from the train on arrival at Carlisle Pier station, Dun Laoghaire, on 6 July 1958, with Irish Customs officers watching as passengers arrive for their ferry journey to Holyhead in Anglesey. On the extreme left (the green building with the oval hole) is the original trainshed dating from 1859 surrounded by the passenger terminal buildings built in 1953. The Pier station was reached by a spur from the main line through Dun Laoghaire, opened by the Dublin and Kingstown Railway in 1834, Kingstown being the original name of Dun Laoghaire until 1921. Carlisle Pier station, named after a former Lord Lieutenant of Ireland, the Earl of Carlisle, was closed in November 1980 and demolished in October 2009. Controversially, the historic trainshed was not spared. *(Charles Firminger)*

This is Bray station, Co Wicklow, on the east coast, photographed by the author from his room in the International Hotel during a family visit to Ireland in August 1966. Horse and donkey-drawn carts were still in evidence in this period and this one has just collected parcels that have arrived by train. The station was built in 1854 by the Dublin and Wicklow Railway and renamed Bray Daly on 10 April 1966. It is located on the Dublin–Rosslare and Arklow routes and was the southern terminus of the DART electric service from its inception in 1984 until the extension to Greystones was opened in 2000, although most of the services to Malahide and Howth start from Bray. The massive 130-bed International Hotel was built in 1862 and destroyed by fire in 1974. *(Author)*

The destination of the carriages being shunted at Dublin Kingsbridge (*see page 113*) had been the Tullow branch, with stations located in Co Wicklow, Co Kildare and Co Carlow. The branch diverged from the GSWR Dublin–Cork mainline at Sallins, but this photograph taken on 16 March 1959 depicts the previous station to the east, Straffan, Co Kildare. Opened in 1848 and closed to passengers on 10 November 1947, the station hardly looks disused twelve years later. The signal cabin on the opposite platform remained open until 1976, after which the station building fell into disrepair and was demolished in the 1980s. *(Charles Firminger)*

This scene is at Baltinglass, Co Wicklow, on the 34¾ mile branch from Sallins to Tullow, Co Carlow and typifies the traffic that extended the life of some of Ireland's rural branch lines. Completed by the GSWR in 1886, the branch closed to passengers on 22 January 1947 but remained open for cattle trains and occasional passenger specials. Here we see the last ever commercial train to operate on the branch beyond Naas, with cattle being loaded on 16 March 1959. By this time the line beyond Baltinglass to Tullow was disused, except for the turning of steam engines on Tullow's turntable, as happened on this occasion when in addition, three permanent way department vehicles were dropped off there for the impending demolition train. *(Charles Firminger)*

With the cattle now loaded, the final train prepares to leave Baltinglass on 16 March 1959 behind GSWR/GSR 101/J15 class 0-6-0 No.171. There were twenty-two cattle trucks in the train, with only six empty. Two loaded ones were detached at Naas and three loaded ones attached. Further cattle trucks were detached at Sallins and beyond. Locomotive No.171 dates from 1874 and was rebuilt in 1933, remaining in service until 1961. The 'flying snail' motif identifies the container lorry on the right as belonging to CIE. *(Charles Firminger)*

This is the same cattle train from Ballinglass, stopping briefly at Harristown on its way to Naas and Sallins, but the formation needs explaining. It is a rare case of an enthusiasts' special being combined with a commercial train. The two passenger coaches and vintage sleeping car are the same ones being shunted on their return at Kingsbridge station on page 113. The train had travelled down on the previous day and the sleeping car was provided as overnight accommodation for the train crew (enthusiasts had to make their own overnight arrangements). As evidenced by this picture, the last official train was a long one, consisting of locomotive No.171, the staff sleeping car, the two passenger coaches for the railfans, sixteen cattle wagons loaded with livestock, six empty cattle wagons and a brake van. Remarkable! *(Charles Firminger)*

Above: The last commercial train from Tulley and Baltinglass has now reached Naas, Co Kildare. A hand reaches out to close the door of the departmental sleeping car, No.224A. This was not, however, the last passenger train to use Naas station. That occurred five days later, on 21 March 1959, when a return racegoers special worked from Kingsbridge for the Navan Races. The branch officially closed on 1 April 1959.
Right: Several withdrawn carriages were being stored in sidings at Naas when the enthusiast special/cattle train called there on 16 March 1959. *(Charles Firminger - both)*

Moving deeper into the south travelling from east to west, we reach Macmine Junction, a station that closed in 1963, although trains still pass the site on their way from Enniscorty to Wexford and Rosslare Harbour. However, the other route that diverged at Macmine is now closed. This went to Palace East where the line split to Bagenalstown to the north and New Ross and Waterford in the south. This picture from the late 1950s depicts an unidentified A class diesel, with its silver livery so grubby that the fleet number on the front is indecipherable, hauling a mixed train that includes an ancient six-wheeled coach. *(Ernie's Railway Archive)*

This photograph was taken at Waterford in July 1957 and depicts CIE railcar Nos.2659/2658 and Park Royal driving trailers Nos.1407/8. The railcars were the last in a batch of sixty built by AEC with Park Royal bodywork between March 1952 and September 1954 and closely resembled the GNR(I)'s railcars. The vehicles seen here were used on the former Waterford and Tramore Railway, an independent company absorbed into the GSR in 1925, and subsequently into CIE. This 7¼ mile line was not connected to any other part of the railway system, so movement of stock to the line was not straightforward. The diesel railcars replaced steam in November 1954 and the line was closed on 31 December 1960. One railcar, No.2624, which later became push-pull unit No.6111 and remained in service until September 1987, is preserved on the Downpatrick & County Down Railway. *(Peter Grace)*

Sugar beet growing and processing was an important industry in Ireland but ceased in 2006, although it might be revived in future. Much of the sugar beet extracted from the ground was transported by rail and this photograph of one such train dates from October 1962. The locomotive is GSWR/GSR 249,351/J9 class 0-6-0 No.249, built at Inchicore in 1912, rebuilt in 1932 and withdrawn in 1963. The class consisted of two batches of four, No.249 belonging to the second batch modified by Richard Maunsell during his short time as Locomotive Superintendent of the GSWR before leaving for the English South Eastern & Chatham Railway in December 1913. The sugar beet train, believed to be the 12.15 pm from Waterford, is standing alongside the mouth of the Colligan River at Dungarvan, presumably heading for the beet factory at Mallow. *(Roy Hobbs)*

Described as a 'boat train' by the American photographer who has just landed at Cobh (formerly Queenstown) in July 1959, this is indeed flattery for an ancient-looking engine and its set of vintage carriages about to head for Cork! The locomotive is GSWR/GSR 101/J15 class 0-6-0 No.179, which clocked up an amazing ninety years of service. Built in 1875 and lasting until 1965, with rebuilds in 1920 and 1933, it is attached to an early outside-framed tender. Cobh station is still open but is much reduced in size, with part of the original station building being used as the Cobh Heritage Centre. *(Donald Nevin)*

The next few pictures are taken at Glanmire Road, Cork, engine shed. This is either CIE No.383 or No.388 – the last number on the smokebox is almost indecipherable and the cab-side number is obscured by the tablet catcher. Both were GSR 372/K1 class 2-6-0s assembled at Broadstone or Inchicore from a kit of parts made at Woolwich Arsenal in England as a means of keeping former munitions workers in employment after the First World War. There were twenty engines in the class, all built with 5ft 6in driving wheels, almost identical to the South Eastern & Chatham Railway's class N, and a further six of GSR 393/K1a class with 6ft driving wheels comparable to the Southern Railway's class U. *(Ernie's Railway Archive)*

This delightful little engine shunting a cattle wagon by the engine shed is ex-Midland & Great Western Railway 0-6-0 tank No.115, *Achill*, built by Kitson & Co of Leeds in 1893. There were twelve members of the class and this locomotive later became GSR No.560 of the J26 class. In 1932 it was fitted with an enlarged bunker, giving an extra one ton of coal capacity, and had its footsteps modified so that they did not protrude. This allowed the locomotive to operate on the 'disconnected' Waterford and Tramore section that had limited clearances. Two other J26s were similarly modified for this line. No.560 was one of three that lasted in service as late as 1963. *(Jim Oatway)*

Withdrawn in 1959 and photographed on 17 March 1961, this diminutive engine was awaiting a preserved future. Initially a static exhibit at Mallow, it has been loaned by Irish Rail to the heritage Downpatrick & County Down Railway in Northern Ireland and was returned to steam in 2006, although it is currently awaiting overhaul. Built as an 0-6-4 tank at Inchicore in 1875, the two pairs of trailing wheels supported a tiny coach that was fixed to the rear of the engine, making it a steam railmotor. The rear wheels and coach were removed in 1915, the locomotive then becoming an 0-6-0. Interestingly, it retained its original smokebox double-doors throughout its life. *(Charles Firminger)*

What better way of celebrating St Patrick's Day than visiting Cork engine shed! Taking water from a heavily lagged water column on 17 March 1961 is ex-Cork, Bandon and South Coast Railway 4-6-0 tank No.8, latterly GSR 463 class No.464, built by Beyer, Peacock in 1920. There were eight of these locomotives, nicknamed 'Bandon Tanks', and this one lasted until 1963, along with No.463, outliving the remainder of the class. In the distance, above the railwayman's head, is 'Pat', the steam-powered vehicle that worked on the coal gantry beside the engine shed (see next page). *(Charles Firminger)*

These are two views of 'Pat' at Cork shed on 17 March 1961. This ex-GSWR standard-gauge steam machine with vertical boiler and cylinders was built at Inchicore in 1884. Scrapped in 1963, it was capable of hauling five full coal wagons along the length of the gantry from Penrose Quay to the locomotive depot. **Far right:** Simmering in the mist on 16 November 1960 at Albert Quay, which involved street running from Glanmire Road, ex-GSWR 201 class 0-6-0 tank No.201 (GSR J11 class), built at Inchicore in 1895, belonged to a class of ten such heavy shunting engines designed by Henry Ivatt, before he moved to the English Great Northern Railway. (Charles Firminger – all)

Above: Here is another photograph of J26 class 0-6-0 tank No.560 (*see page 129*), this time working at Albert Quay in October 1962. **Right:** Built for the Kerry branch in 1894, No.36 belonged to a class of six 2-4-2 tanks (GSWR 33/GSR F6) and is seen in June 1957, its year of withdrawal, at open-air Albert Quay shed (lucky locomotives could shelter under the overbridge!).
(Roy Hobbs; Nick Nicolson/The Transport Treasury)

For a last visit to Cork city, station pilot No.464 (*see page 131*) stands alongside diesel No.A29, which has arrived at Glanmire Road (now renamed Kent) station with a boat train from Rosslare Harbour on 18 March 1961. *(Charles Firminger)*

For this and the next three pictures, we remain in Co Cork and view part of the former Cork, Bandon and South Coast Railway (CBSCR) that terminated at Albert Quay. Originally called the Cork & Bandon Railway, the name was changed in recognition of the various extensions that culminated in the railway having five separate branches, serving Kinsale, Courtmacsherry, Clonakilty, Baltimore and Bantry. This photograph was taken on 18 November 1960 at Crossbarry, previously called Kinsale Junction, and shows CIE 201 class diesel locomotive No.C216 shunting. These West Cork lines closed on Easter Saturday, 1 April 1961. *(Charles Firminger)*

The shiny water crane stands idle for No.C216's visit on 18 November 1960 to Bandon, the second station west of Crossbarry. The brick station building dating from 1894, replacing an earlier structure on the site of the goods yard, is visible behind the diesel. The new building was located on an island platform and survives today, but the signal box and goods yard have made way for a new road. Built in 1956, No.C216 was renumbered B216 after receiving a replacement, more powerful engine along with the other thirty-three members of the class. Following withdrawal by CIE, the locomotive was one of six sold to Northern Ireland Railways, entering service in 1986, but was only in service for eight years and was scrapped in 1997. *(Charles Firminger)*

Left: Ex-MGWR E class 0-6-0 tank No.107, *Robin* (later GSR class 551/J26 No.552), hauls a sugar beet train between Skeaf and Ballinascarthy on the former CBSCR Courtmacsherry branch on 19 November 1960. Built by Kitson's in 1891, this veteran was not withdrawn until 1963.
Above: Retaining its original cab and bunker (unlike No.560 on pages 129 and 134) but having lost its metal number plate, No.552 stands with a wagonload of sugar beet at Ballinascarthy, junction for the Courtmacsherry and Clonakilty branches. *(Charles Firminger – both)*

Left: Moving into Co Kerry, this is Kenmare, terminus of a branch from Headford Junction, a subsequently abandoned station on the existing Mallow–Tralee line. The branch closed on 1 February 1960. The locomotive is GSWR/GSR 101/J15 class No.156, built at Inchicore in 1871, rebuilt in 1935 and withdrawn in 1961. **Above:** One of the intermediate stations on the Kenmare branch was Loo Bridge, photographed here on 7 November 1959 with unmodernised J15 No.133 in charge of a Kenmare-bound mixed train. In October 2015, the renovated station building was advertised for sale with an asking price of 210,000 euros.
(Ernie's Railway Archive; Charles Firminger)

On 17 November 1959, J15 class 0-6-0 No.133 is about to leave Headford Junction for Kenmare as an express from Dublin to Killarney and Tralee arrives. The station nameboard's reference to Parknasilla is to the former GSWR's hotel overlooking Kenmare Bay at Sneem.
Right: Moving across to Mallow, Co Cork, where the Tralee–Mallow line (now closed east of Mallow to Waterford) meets the Dublin–Cork mainline, one of the trio of magnificent GSR 800 class 4-6-0s, No.801, *Macha*, stands by the coaling stage at Mallow shed on 5 June 1961.

(Charles Firminger – two; J.L. Stevenson)

We now journey to Limerick Junction in Co Tipperary, where the Waterford–Limerick line crosses the Dublin–Cork main line on the level (that is, by a diamond crossing). In this view, GSWR/GSR 301/D11 class 4-4-0 No.301 (built at Inchicore in 1900 and originally named *Victoria*) stands alongside the South signal cabin in June 1957. Rebuilt in 1931, this locomotive outlived the other four D11s and was officially withdrawn in 1960, although it was surprisingly resurrected for service in spring 1961 and ended up as a stationary boiler at Inchicore.
(Nick Nicolson/The Transport Treasury)

This Sulzer Bo-Bo locomotive, completed in January 1950 at Inchicore as No.1100 and renumbered B113 in 1957, was Ireland's first mainline diesel and is now preserved at Cultra. Unlike many of CIE's later diesels, it did not need to be re-engined in later life but did suffer braking problems that were eventually rectified, albeit it at the end of its working career. Belonging to a class of only two locomotives and withdrawn in January 1975, B113 is seen here on 4 July 1958 at Limerick Junction. The train could have been an excellent example of CIE's modern image, had it not been for the inclusion of two cattle wagons in the formation! *(Charles Firminger)*

Left: This delightful station called Oola (named after the local village), photographed on 4 July 1958, was one of the now abandoned intermediate stops between Limerick Junction and Limerick on the former Waterford & Limerick Railway. The station opened in 1848 and closed on 9 September 1963. **Above:** A scene at Limerick engine shed in October 1962 depicting newly outshopped 2600 class AEC railcar No.2618 and GSWR/GSR 101/J15 class 0-6-0 No.198, the latter receiving final checks before re-entry into traffic. The overhaul at Limerick Works of this veteran from 1899 provided a further three years of service. *(Charles Firminger – two; Roy Hobbs)*

We now visit the West Clare Railway (WCR), Ireland's last passenger-carrying narrow-gauge line, connecting with the Limerick–Galway line at Ennis, Co Clare. The WCR, which opened in 1887, ran to Moyasta Junction where it split, one branch going to Kilrush and the other to Kilkee. It was absorbed by the GSR in 1925 and by CIE in 1945, closing on 31 January 1961. The line had a large stud of motive power, consisting of eighteen steam locomotives and seven diesels, including four Walker railcars such as the one shown here at Kilkee on 23 March 1957. The station building is now a private residence. *(Paul de Beer/Online Transport Archive)*

This is a view of the WCR's second western terminus, Kilrush, with a Walker railcar at the platform on 18 August 1958. Again, the station building, built in 1892, survives today as a private residence. A preservation society, the West Clare Railway, runs trains over a two mile section from Moyasta Junction and hopes eventually to reach Kilkee. The heritage railway possesses the sole surviving WCR steam locomotive, No.5, *Slieve Callan*, which was previously a static exhibit at Ennis station and was returned to steam in 2009. In addition, the Irish Traction Society, set up to preserve Irish diesel locomotives, has located some of its stock on standard-gauge track at Moyasta Junction. *(J.L. Stevenson)*

Here is Ennis station in 1966, with 141 class Bo-Bo diesel No.171 heading south on a freight. This locomotive was built by General Motors of Illinois, USA, in 1962 and was the last of the class of thirty-seven to remain in service, ending up as the Inchicore Works shunter before being retired in December 2013. The West Clare Railway's terminus, including an engine shed and yard, was on the far left of the main span of the footbridge and exited under the road bridge behind the last goods wagon, the aperture having been closed up by 1966. For its passenger trains the WCR used the platform face on the far left, fenced off in this picture. One of Ennis' currently protected structures is the cast-iron water column (devoid of hose) standing close to the platform edge beyond the footbridge. *(Ernie's Railway Archive)*

The GSR's (indeed, arguably Ireland's) most prestigious steam locomotives were the three powerful 800/B1a class 4-6-0s built in 1939-40 for the Dublin-Cork route. These three-cylinder machines were the first in Ireland to be built with a double blastpipe and double chimney, although this arrangement does not seem to have been entirely satisfactory because one (No.801 – *see page 143*) ran with a single chimney from 1954 until withdrawal. The proliferation of mainline diesels on CIE from the mid-1950s saw these fine locomotives increasingly demoted from passenger to freight duties, as exemplified in this photograph of the pioneer, No.800, *Maeve*, on a horse van train at Thurles in July 1957. It is noticeable that No.800, which is now preserved at Cultra, does not have its smokebox door disfigured by additional brackets as carried by No.801. *(Peter Grace)*

Above: GSWR/GSR 101/J15 class 0-6-0 No.104 is assembling a freight train in this view at Thurles on 12 May 1962. This locomotive is a good representative of the class' longevity, being built in January 1873 and subsequently clocking up ninety-two years of service, although this is not a record as No.151 managed ninety-seven years and thirteen lasted at least ninety years! The success of these 'maids of all work' is demonstrated by the fact that the 119 class members were built over a long period (1866-1903) and withdrawn over an even longer period (1885-1965). Two have been preserved, both by the RPSI: No.184 (a reasonably original-looking one) and No.186 in rebuilt state like the one pictured here.

Right: No.C228 enters Portarlington, Co Laois, on 4 July 1958 with a train from Dublin that includes two vintage CIE carriages, No.1119 and No.1316. Portarlington, on the Dublin–Cork mainline, is also the junction for the Athlone/Galway line. *(Jim Oatway; Charles Firminger – two)*

Above: Mullingar, Co Westmeath, is on the Dublin–Sligo line and also on the Dublin–Longford route. In addition, there was a line to Athlone and onwards to Galway, but services now operate via Portarlington and the Mullingar–Athlone link has been mothballed. These scenes depict Mullingar locomotive depot in July 1957. The buildings attached to the shed were used by the MGWR as offices and accommodation for railway workers. The shed is now occupied by the RPSI's carriage department and the turntable is occasionally used for steam railtours.

Right: Archaic-looking ex-MGWR LM class 0-6-0, *Nephin*, (latterly GSR J18 class No.592) shunts in front of the engine shed. This locomotive was built by Kitson's in 1895 and withdrawn in 1962. *(Peter Grace – both)*

Athlone originally had two rival railway stations: the MGWR one on the west side of the River Shannon serving Dublin Broadstone–Galway via Mullingar and the GSWR one on the east side of the Shannon reaching Galway via a branch off the Dublin–Cork mainline. At the MGWR station there were two separate engine sheds – a small one very close to the station and a larger one slightly farther on – which is the location of this picture dating from July 1957. Taking centre stage is C 204, one of the 34 C class (later 201 class) diesels built by Metropolitan Vickers of Manchester and designed for branch-line passenger and freight work. The locomotive later became B 204 (and then plain 204) following the replacement of its unsatisfactory Crossley engine with a General Motors one. Only a year old, No.C 204's initial silver livery is not yet looking its worst. *(Peter Grace)*

For those readers who have almost given up hope of seeing a 2-4-0 tender engine, here is one! This is ex-MGWR K class No.28, *Clara*, (GSR 650/G2 class No.654), built at Broadstone in 1897, one of twenty such locomotives. This view shows No.654 in June 1962 (shortly before its withdrawal) approaching Dunsandle, the only intermediate station on the nine mile branch to Lochrea, Co Galway, which ran from Attymon Junction, on the Dublin–Galway line west of Athlone. The Lochrea and Attymon Light Railway Co. opened the branch in 1890 and it closed to passengers on 3 November 1975, making it Ireland's last passenger-carrying rural railway. Attymon station remains open. *(Roy Hobbs)*

Left: G2 class 2-4-0 No.654, complete with photogenic train crew, leaves Dunsandle for Lochrea. **Above:** By coincidence, here is an engine that was once named *Dunsandle*: ex-MGWR L class (GSR 573/J18 class) 0-6-0 No.574, built at Inchicore in 1891 and rebuilt with a Belpaire boiler in 1940. It is seen at Ballaghaderreen, Co Roscommon, on a mixed train from Kilfree Junction early in the morning of the last day of passenger services on the branch, 2 February 1963. Today, the unique rough stone station building lies derelict and a health centre stands on the site of the water tower and engine shed. *(Roy Hobbs)*

Ex-MGWR K class 2-4-0 No.13, *Rapid*, (GSR 650/G2 class No.659), built at Broadstone in 1893, awaits departure at Ballaghaderreen with the first train of the day to Kilfree Junction in June 1959. Goods traffic, which was predominantly agricultural, was the mainstay of the branch and latterly there were only three passenger workings per day. The G2 2-4-0s were competent performers on local and branch passenger trains and six of the twenty built remained in service until 1961-63, outliving all other 2-4-0 tender engines in the British Isles, if not in the world.
(Roy Hobbs)

The Ballaghaderreen branch from Kilfree Junction, a now-closed station on the Dublin–Sligo mainline, had two intermediate stations, Edmondstown and Island Road, both of which have now been converted into dwellings. This picture shows G2 class 2-4-0 No.653 (ex-MGWR No.19, *Spencer*) standing at Edmondstown on a mixed train from Kilfree Junction. An unusual bi-directional signal can be seen behind the noticeboard. Standing on the locomotive, smartly dressed as ever in his guard's uniform, is Christie Plunkett, whose wife worked in the ticket office at Ballaghaderreen and who also operated the signals and points, the equipment being housed in the station building.
(Ernie's Railway Archive)

Standing beside the water tower at Belturbet, Co Cavan, on 8 June 1957 is GNR(I) JT class 2-4-2 tank No.91. This locomotive, belonging to a class of six built at Dundalk Works, entered service in 1902 as No.13, *Tulip*. The remaining five were withdrawn before the GNR Board was dissolved in 1958, including No.93, *Sutton*, which is preserved at Cultra, but No.91 was acquired by CIE and was not withdrawn until 1963. In this picture No.91 is resting between duties on the branch train to Ballyhaise on the GNR(I)'s Clones to Cavan line. Belturbet closed to passengers in 1957 and to freight in 1959 but, after years of dereliction, most of the railway buildings have been restored and the station building is now a museum. As well as being on the GNR(I), Belturbet was also the eastern terminus of the narrow-gauge Cavan & Leitrim Railway (CLR), which also closed in 1959. *(Paul de Beer/Online Transport Archive)*

Our journey around the Republic of Ireland ends with a visit to the CLR, which was a neighbour of the cross-border County Donegal Railway and the Sligo, Leitrim and Northern Counties Railway covered in the Northern Ireland section of the book. In 1887, the Cavan, Leitrim and Roscommon Light Railway and Tramway Company opened a line linking the GNR(I) at Belturbet with the Midland and Great Western Railway at Dromod in Co Leitrim. The second station west of Belturbet was Ballyconnell, the location of this photograph of a train hauled by Neilson, Reid 2-4-2 tank No.12L. Over the years the C&LR's locomotive fleet was increased by the purchase of second-hand engines including four from the Cork, Blackrock and Passage Railway after its closure in 1932 and which, like the CLR, had become part of Great Southern Railways in 1925. The four acquired locomotives, including No.12L, were all built by Neilson, Reid & Co in 1900. Two lasted until closure in 1959 but neither survives. *(Paul de Beer/Online Transport Archive)*

Roughly halfway between Belturbet and Dromond was Ballinamore. In the year following the opening of the line in 1887, this station became a junction when a tramway using the existing railway locomotives was built from Ballinamore to Arigna in Co Roscommon. Ballinamore was the headquarters of the CLR, where this picture of 4-4-0 tank No.2L, *Kathleen,* on a freight was taken in October 1953. No.2L was one of the eight original locomotives built by Robert Stephenson & Co of Newcastle for the opening of the line and is now preserved at Cultra. Another of the original engines, No.3L, *Lady Edith*, also survives and is exhibited in the New Jersey Museum of Transportation in America. The station buildings at Ballinamore survive today as a school. *(W.E. Robertson/Online Transport Archive)*

This view at Ballinamore, also dating from October 1953, shows the engine shed on the right and the CLR's only footbridge in the centre. The locomotive on the left is 2-6-0 tank No.3T, originally built by the Hunslet Engine Co in 1889 for the Tralee & Dingle Light Railway in Co Kerry (hence the 'T' suffix) and acquired by the CLR in 1941 following the cessation of passenger services on that line in 1939 (final closure was in 1953 following withdrawal of the monthly cattle train). In the centre of the picture is No.2L, *Kathleen* (see previous picture). *(W.E. Robertson/Online Transport Archive)*

2-6-0 tank No.4T approaches Mohill station on the section of line from Ballinamore to Dromod with a loaded coal train. Dromod station is now preserved and is the headquarters of the heritage CLR, which operates over a quarter of a mile of track. No.4T was built by Kerr, Stuart & Co in 1903 for the Tralee & Dingle Light Railway and was photographed on 5 July 1958. The Mex sign on the adjacent road is another reminder of the past. The name originated with the Mexican Eagle Petroleum company, which was taken over by Shell in 1921. However, the Irish assets were excluded and sold to the owners of the company whose brand name since 1972 is Maxol, this name replacing older brand names such as Mex. *(Charles Firminger)*

Moving to the Arigna branch, which was largely a roadside tramway, the second station after Ballinamore was Cornabrone, the setting for this charming scene on 5 July 1958. CIE's ownership of the C&L after absorbing the GSR in 1948 is evidenced by the 'flying snail' motif on the carriage. The locomotive is ex-Tralee & Dingle 2-6-0 No.3T. Slightly larger 2-6-2 tank No.5T has fortunately been saved, making it the only ex-Tralee & Dingle engine in existence. Bought by the Steamtown Museum, Vermont, USA following the C&L's closure, it was repatriated in 1989 and was returned to steam by the heritage Tralee and Blennerville Steam Railway Group, but is currently dismantled. C&L Nos.5-8 were originally fitted with side plates covering the wheels for use on the tramway. *(Charles Firminger)*

Above: This is another shot of 2-6-0 tank No.3T on the Arigna branch, this time on the curve at Kilturbrid station just in front of the level crossing, the lamp from which is visible on the extreme right. Today the building is a private house. **Right:** We are now one station away from Arigna and there seems to be activity on the platform at Drumshanbo as a member of the footplate crew stands atop No.3T while it takes water. The water tower and station buildings survive today but are divided by a road that occupies the trackbed at this point.
(Charles Firminger – both).

Left: No.3T has now disposed of its wagons and is about to bring its single carriage into Arigna. **Above:** We have now reached Arigna station and ex-Tralee & Dingle 2-6-2 tank No.5T is about to depart with a loaded coal train. The mines at Arigna were the mainstay of the railway's traffic, to which the tramway was extended in 1920, with coal being carried to the standard-gauge railheads at Belturbet and Dromond for use across Ireland. However, with the building of a coal-fired power station in 1958 at Arigna, to which much of the mine's coal was diverted, and the greater convenience of road haulage, the C&L's transportation services were no longer needed and Ireland's last exclusively steam narrow-gauge railway ceased operation on 31 March 1959. *(Charles Firminger – both)*

With exactly two weeks to go before closure of the CLR, No.3T stands ready to leave Arigna on 17 March 1959 with a passenger train. The carriage, providing first and second class accommodation, is an elderly brake composite with a verandah at each end. When one of the balcony coaches was hauled by an original CLR locomotive with full-sized 'cow catcher', the resulting train had a distinctly 'Wild West' appearance to it! *(Paul de Beer/Online Transport Archive)*

Moving from one CLR terminus to another, this is Belturbet (featured also on page 162) where there was a joint CLR/GNR station. No.12L (ex- Cork, Blackrock & Passage Railway No. 6) is standing beside the CLR water tower on 8 June 1957. The GNR had its own, rather taller stone water tower located closer to the station, the latter being visible in the background between the GNR goods vans. The black building immediately to the left of the locomotive's cab is the transfer shed where freight was physically moved between the different gauged wagons. *(Paul de Beer/Online Transport Archive)*

We return to Ballinamore for a view of two former Tralee & Dingle (T&D) locomotives standing outside the engine shed in October 1953. In front of No 4T (already seen on page 166) is No 5T, still carrying its previous owner's boiler-mounted bell. This 2-6-2 tank locomotive was built by the Hunslet Engine Company in 1892 and was moved from the T&D in 1949 to Inchicore Works before arriving at the CLR in the following year. When the CLR closed in 1959 No.5L went to the USA but was repatriated in 1989, returning to its original line under the auspices of the heritage Tralee & Blennerville Railway and restored to running order. However, this sole surviving T&D locomotive has not operated since 2006 and the line is currently defunct, but will hopefully reopen. *(W E Robertson/Online Transport Archive)*

Index